The New Black Power

A Collection of Essays by The People's Scholar, Dr. Boyce Watkins

Boyce Watkins, Ph.D.

The New Black Power: *A Collection of Essays by The People's Scholar, Dr. Boyce Watkins*

Your Black World Store
3750 Hacks Cross Road, Suite 102-137
Memphis, TN 38125
www.shopyourblackworld.net
store@yourblackworld.net

Ordering Information:
Quantity sales. Special discounts are available on quantity purchases by corporations, associations, and others. For details, contact the publisher at the address above.

Orders by U.S. trade bookstores and wholesalers. Please contact the Your Black World Store: Tel: (315) 308-1029 or visit www.shopyourblackworld.net.

Printed in the United States of America

First Printing, 2016

ISBN-13: 978-1536805598
ISBN-10: 1536805599

TABLE OF CONTENT

Introduction

After finishing my Ph.D. in Finance many years ago, I was proud to have been labeled as a thinker. After spending well over a decade studying between 7 and 10 hours a day, every single day of the week, the world convinced me that I had accomplished something.

But while I'd certainly mastered high-level mathematics, mind-numbing statistical analysis and the most complex theories of finance, my education was missing one critical component: Training on how to become a strong and productive member of the African American community.

So, while the universities I attended were certainly equipped to teach me how to become a financial scientist, they were woefully inadequate at preparing me to become a black man. In fact, through all of the years I spent in college, graduate school and doctoral work, I never even once had a single black professor at any time, in any field.

This was the foundation of my brainwashing.

I spent the bulk of my thirties unlearning the vast majority of everything that the racist American educational system taught me about myself. I had to rediscover myself, love myself and not be afraid to be myself. It was only after this period of intense self-reflection that I was able to emerge as an effective and relevant scholar for my community.

I measure success in the black community, for the most part, in one way: Your contribution to the community from which you came. Receiving awards, money and validation from your oppressor means almost nothing to me. Catering to a White Supremacist system while abandoning those you love is like a man feeding every child in the neighborhood, while letting his own kids starve to death.

Black people are the economic and political engine on which everyone else is able to feed to their advantage: We get Democrats elected to office; corporations have earned trillions in profits on our backs; the NCAA robs our greatest athletes and their poverty-stricken mothers; our school systems are filled with black kids being trained by white women from the suburbs; American prisons have become fat from black slave labor.

Being black often means that we are forced to have ridiculous conversations to defend clearly valid points on non-issues, such as whether or not the community deserves reparations or whether a police officer should be able to kill a black man without fear of indictment.

The world is filled with double standards that run along racial lines, largely because this country's leaders have never seen us as fully human. They love us like the family pet, who sits as an irreplaceable member of the household, but will be shot to death if he ever harms a family member or forgets his place in the hierarchy. The black experience in America is a 400-year story of domestic violence, racial terror, passionate resistance and miraculous triumph. They can't kill us, even though they've tried on several occasions and it almost seems that they are now becoming fearful that we might try to kill them.

Most of us aren't interested in killing white people, but nearly all of us are absolutely determined to slaughter white supremacy. I am hopeful that conscientious whites will join us in this struggle because once the battle is over, we will remember the silence of our so-called "friends." As we are in the midst of one of the greatest social awakenings of the last 200 years, there has never been a better time to be black.

This book covers the thoughts that I've shared publicly over the last several years. I've seen extraordinary changes occur in this country and also in my personal life since I began my journey of public scholarship many years ago.

Through the years, I've always stood by every word I've uttered, even when I made a fool out of myself. I've always believed in telling the truth, even if it's painful, embarrassing or might get you killed. So, everything I write for you is from the heart because I don't know how to do it any other way.

I appreciate those who've stood by me through the years, namely my brother Lawrence, my wonderful mother Robin, the father who raised me and my incredibly loyal assistant Shauntay. My daughters have been amazing, as have my God children, filling a void in my heart that kept me up at night for many years.

Thank you to my mentors, Dr. Tommy Whittler, Dr. Cornel West, Dr. Claud Anderson, Dr. Julianne Malveaux and Minister Louis Farrakhan. Thank you to my team at Your Black World and The Black Business School, who've tolerated me when I am my sloppiest and most tyrannical.

Finally, I truly appreciate the many millions of you who appreciate thoughtful analysis in a world that seems to have become addicted to ignorance.

Black people are waking up, standing up and rising up. There is nothing anyone can do to stop it.

Boyce Watkins, Ph.D.
The People's Scholar

Chapter 1

The Black Celebrity as Purveyor of Black Culture

Dr. Boyce: Does Hip Hop Influence Young People? Just Ask Adolph Hitler or any Good Psychologist

Some say that hip hop music is as harmless as a Robert De Niro gangster film or something that you see on TV. The problem with this analogy is that hip-hop is fueled by a type of authenticity that you don't need in Hollywood. De Niro will gladly tell you "I'm not a real gangster, I just play one in the movies." Lil Wayne can't pretend to be a gangster; he's expected to be a real one. This enhances hip-hop's ability to promote an entire lifestyle that goes deeper than simply producing songs that you want to shake your b**t to. Every teenager wants to be cool, and an easy way to be cool is to emulate cool people. There is no one cooler in high school than your favorite hip-hop artist: If the rapper Drake and Barack Obama appeared at the same high school on the same day, the president would have no audience.

Someone, during our Hot 97 conversation, asked "given that most of the consumers of hip hop are white suburban kids, why are they not impacted by the images?" I've taught on majority white college campuses for the last 20 years, and I've noticed the fascination that many white students have with black men from "the hood." It's not that they want to be like them (they would never trade their suburban lifestyles for life in the hood), but they see them as cool, exotic African creatures that they will gladly pay money to see, but never bring home to daddy, recommend for a job or respect as an intelligent human being. To some extent, rappers are like musical call-girls—a man might really enjoy his time with a prostitute and show loyal patronage for her services. But he never truly respects her as anything other than a way to fulfill a specific set of desires.

Non-black kids are simply being ENTERTAINED by images of blackness being presented by the hip hop artist. The white kids are not always interested in trying to be black, they just enjoy the excitement of hearing the stories and seeing the images (they want to know what it's like to be a "n***a in Paris" and are fascinated by black men with big chains and tattoos). The black kids are the ones who look at the black artist and are tempted to say, "That's the kind of person I am supposed to be" (even when their parents tell them otherwise). The image is one that is built off the authenticity granted by "the hood," sold to white Americans and often emulated by black youth either seeking to themselves make money by selling their blackness to white people or to gain the same kind of hood respect that the artist gets for being the alpha male.

Some say that good parenting can easily overcome the impact of negative hip hop. That's an insult to good parents everywhere whose kids are being heavily influenced by this music. Their child might not go out and kill anyone, but they certainly gain a distorted perception of alcohol/drug use, s****l decisions and the necessity to run to the club every weekend, with much of this influence coming from the cultural norms being created around them. I knew a teen who loved to listen to the Gucci Mane song "Wasted," (which boasts about waking up with a liquor bottle in your hand) who then went to college and nearly died of alcohol poisoning before dropping out. It was by watching this child's influences all through high school that I could clearly see that her perception of college life as a big party was heavily impacted by the music that she and her friends listened to.

The bottom line is that negative commercialized hip hop is not harmless. That's like saying that Adolph Hitler's *Mein Kampf* was just a harmless little book or that the Bible and gospel music have no impact on Christianity.

There is a reason that whenever a country invades another one, one of the first things they do is destroy radio and TV stations. It's because when you control the minds of a group of people, you are controlling the people themselves. When corporate behemoths are flooding urban airwaves with messages that serve as a blueprint for black male self-destruction, they are not creating an army of strong black fathers, husbands and scholars. Instead, they are creating an even larger army of pants-sagging, blunt-smoking, tattooed-up, uneducated, STD-infected, impoverished thugs who partner with an already oppressive system to destroy themselves and their families (don't even pretend that you don't know a brother who's chosen this to be his identity, even when he had other options).

Yes, there is much accountability to spread around as politicians maintain inferior schools, fuel the prison industrial complex, turn a blind eye to rampant urban violence and ignore black unemployment (I write on these issues regularly). You can also hold that same system accountable for funding the music that encourages these men to give up on their lives and seek to either kill one another or kill themselves via s****l irresponsibility and drug/alcohol abuse.

But when the oppression gets this deep and insidious, it always takes two to tango. The system is the pimp and our community is the ho, and these relationships don't work unless both parties are playing their role

Dr. Boyce: Does Reality TV Inspire a Generation of Young, Female Bullies?

I find myself consistently fascinated at how angry and ugly women can be on Vh-1 reality shows. Rather than attempting to understand the inner beauty that makes a human being lovable, too many seem to think that attraction comes down to long hair, a short dress and a shapely backside.

The women on these reality shows actually scare me. They seem determined to remain consistently angry at someone about something. There is almost nothing that would make me proud to have them as daughters, sisters or mothers in my own family. The idea that these women are serving as role models for an entire generation of young women is sad, sick and disturbing.

"Unfortunately I do think that reality TV has spawned a whole culture of bullying," Phaedra Parks told the Associated Press. "I believe that the behavior you see on reality TV does not exactly exemplify how adults should be conducting themselves."

Many reality TV shows, most specifically the *Real Housewives, Basketball Wives and Love and HipHop* franchises, are being accused of promoting bullying among young girls who are still learning how to resolve their disputes with one another. Young women may find it fashionable and powerful to engage in consistent outbursts of anger, intimidation and name-calling in order to achieve dominance, rather than attempting to make peace and support one another.

Kandi Burress of the *Real Housewives of Atlanta* does not agree with my assessment. "A lot of people try to find reasons or ways to blame people or situations for their grief or sadness," Burruss said. "Personally, I think reality TV is a mimic of what's happening in real life, not the other way around. People have always had arguments, and there's always been cliques."

Even though reality television didn't invent bullying, it certainly glorified, elevated, and mass marketed the concept. I was once forced by a woman I dated to watch shows like *Basketball Wives* every night (the things we do for love). I figured that watching the show might be good research for the things I write about, so I agreed. I admit that I spent much of my time in awe, wondering how women could be so treacherous toward one another.

As I observed the show, I noticed that exactly 100% of the promotional segments featured some kind of confrontation: In every case, someone was being physically attacked, verbally assaulted, double crossed or gossiped into the ground. The women seemed to form glamor mafia factions against one another, always planning their next invasion. I can't imagine the stress of living under that kind of pressure.

Terrie Williams, author of *Black Pain*, once made a profound statement to me: "Hurt people, tend to hurt people," she said. So, when I think about the women on *Basketball Wives*, I wonder what kind of pain they've experienced to make them so determined to mutilate the soul of another human being. When you consider how many women of color have had their hearts broken by the first man in their life (daddy), it puts this rampant emotional violation into context.

When I see shows like *Basketball Wives*, I think about my own daughters and behavior I'd seen from them when they were at their worst. When one makes the connection, you can't help but see the direct impact that these shows can have on impressionable young minds. It seems ironic that at the highest levels of government, we are seeking to bring bullying to an end (even criminalizing it), yet on television, we are actually encouraging it.

Since s*x and violence always sell, there's no point in expecting these shows to go off the air. But perhaps we can turn the television off when our kids are watching this kind of stuff, and talk to one another about being loving and supporting, rather than trying to find someone to smack upside the head. It's d**n stressful to be angry all the time, and there's nothing appealing about an 'ignant' woman always looking for a fight.

We have GOT to do better.

Is Trinidad James an Artist or a Buffoon? Dr. Chistopher Emdin Discusses

Dr. Boyce Watkins had a conversation about the impact that hip-hop is having on the youth who listen to it. To add to the conversation, he invited Dr. Christopher Emdin to weigh in on the conversation about what rappers like Trinidad James are actually doing to young people when they release records full of destructive messages. The interview is below:

Dr. Watkins: Hi. I'm Dr. Boyce Watkins from YourBlackWorld.com. Last week I was in New York City and I stopped by a radio station, in the City, called Power 105.1, which is a hip-hop station. One of my buddies is one of the hosts on the show called the Breakfast Club. His name is Charlamagne Tha God. So, I stopped through to talk to Charlamagne and we were talking about some of this nonsense with BET and whether or not it's affecting our kids and stuff like that. I asked Charlamagne, "What do you think about this guy, this new rapper, Trinidad James?"

Charalamagne said: "Oh, yeah. Trinidad was here right before you got here." I said, "I'm so happy I didn't cross paths with him on my way in the door because I think that might have been my first arrest for assault because I probably would have tried to beat this brother down. His music just bothers me so much. But, then again, maybe I'm just a hater because he's got more money than me."

To gain greater perspective about this, I wanted to bring in one of my buddies who is also one of the scholars who I respect the most in the country, Dr. Christopher Emdin. He's not just a Professor of Education at Columbia University, which is impressive enough; but he's also a very, very good hip-hop artist. I've literally seen him bust freestyle in front of a group of high school kids and at the same time talk to them about how the power of hip-hop can be used to teach them science. So, I've got Dr. Emdin on the line.

Dr. Boyce: How are you doing today, brother?

Dr. Emdin: I'm doing well, man. I'm really appreciative that you gave me the opportunity to share some insight on this situation with Trinidad James. He's blowing up overnight.

Dr. Boyce: Yeah. He really is. Is it true he's been rapping for about 8 or 9 months?

Dr. Emdin: The interview narrative has been about 8 or 9 months but I think he's been rapping a little bit longer. I vividly remember actually being in Atlanta about a year and a half ago and I was talking with some young people. Some of them were saying, "Yo. Trinidad James is next. Trinidad James is the truth." So, I think he's actually been rapping a little bit longer than the narrative that's being put out to the public. His fan base has been there for quite a while.

Dr. Boyce: Really. Okay.

Dr. Emdin: Yes, sir.

Dr. Boyce: So, Trinidad just got a deal with Def Jam Records. It's so interesting because I'm kind of, mentally, in that space. I literally had an hour and a half long meeting yesterday with Russell Simmons talking about bringing in hip-hop artists to support our campaign on mass incarceration. You're also in that space because you just finished an extraordinary event with Gza from the Wu Tang Clan on how to use hip-hop to teach science. So, what is your take on the legitimacy now – or the perceived legitimacy of this artist who is producing music that many people might call straight coonery and buffoonery?

Dr. Emdin: See, this is my take and I want to be very, very clear. I do not blame Trinidad James for his overnight success. I don't blame Trinidad James for the fact that he is on every radio station across the country. Nor do I blame him for the fact that he has become an overnight phenomena. What I do blame is a record company that will sign this artist, support this artist, give him money, and continue in this trajectory or piggy back off of this underground success he's made at the expense of promoting a caricature of blackness. I don't blame the brother. The black experience has its nuances. There is somebody who Trinidad James raps to and for. Just like there's somebody that Gza raps to and for. There's a wide array of that. There's intellectual rap. There's street rap. There's pop and molly rap. I don't advocate for the negative but I realize that it exists.

In my view, my issue is not with the artist himself. My issue is with a public and with a corporate hip-hop system. We call it hip-hop. We call it something—an institution that's supposed to advocate for our culture only identifying the negative caricature and making sure that that becomes what the picture is of the entire culture. That's what I have a problem with. I have a problem with radio stations choosing to take Trinidad James and put him on their station in New York City or across the globe as what is the newest and hottest artist in the country. Because they have the power to be able to identify another artist that is much more talented and perhaps has a different robust subject matter, and make that person be the picture of hip-hop.

So, I don't blame the man. The man that's speaking based on his experiences, or his circumstances, or what he sees in Atlanta every day, or his self-construction, however flawed that may be. I won't critique that one publicly. I would like to have a conversation with him about why that is how he constructs who he is; why it is that he sees the world this way. I've heard interviews with the brother. He's actually quite articulate. So, I'd like to talk to him about, "Why don't you pull forth more of the complexity of who you are into your music?" That's conversation between me and Trinidad James or anybody who loves hip-hop or loves black men and wants to see them be more then what they are portrayed to be. That's a conversation between us and Trinidad.

My critique is not him. My critique is the system. My critique is the corporate system that allows us to force-feed this nonsense to our young people. My critique is of the fact that we are now at a point where we are advocating for these who are spitting nursery school rhymes as if that's complex hip-hop. I don't think Trinidad James is a product of isolation. He didn't come out of nowhere. Trinidad James is the ancestor of Rick Ross. Rick Ross has a nursery school rhyme and he pauses and says, "uh." And then, Trinidad James says, "Hot tamale, I'm sweating, whoo." That's the same cadence. It's the basic baseline nursery rhyme cadence. You know, Trinidad James is the evolution of Rick Ross. And, there will be many more incarnations of that simplistic rap if we don't get to the point where we start critiquing it and saying, 'Hey, Company, there's a brother right now, called "X", who is spitting hip-hop on a consistent basis about every social dynamic of our time. Every social construction where he talks about black maleness, politics, the media, and corporate entity, he talks about all these things that really affect black men but you're not going to offer him a deal. You won't give him the debility.'

He won't get spins on 105.1 or Hot 97. Then you blame the audience like the audience is asking for it. The audience isn't asking for it. The audience is asking for complexity and blackness. You take that as the message you want to show us and then you blame us because we're the ones consuming.

We're consuming because you're feeding it."

And this is why I go back to what a great man once said: *It is that time that we turn off the radio, turn off the BS, and we get to the point where we start supporting artists who speak to and for us.* And when we have those artists that don't do that, we critique them individually; we critique them personally. We have a conversation about them because those brothers are hurt. They're lonely. They're speaking those narratives because they're still trying to find themselves. I hear Trinidad James. I don't get angry at the brother. I get angry at the circumstances that allowed him to feel like this is the only way that he can get some visibility.

So, where we are right now is to really focus on the entities who push these messages upon us. That take one artist out of Atlanta and put him on a National billboard. And the question we have to ask ourselves is not why Trinidad James is creating that rap, it's why is the public and the company and the record label and MTV and Viacom and Clear Channel and 105.1, 97.1, or whatever radio station it is that you're listening to throughout the country, singling him out as what we should be showing our young people as an example. That's who I blame, not the man.

Dr. Boyce: I'm in complete agreement with you. And, I'll say this: anybody who hasn't seen Trinidad James' video has got to check out his song. The song that made him successful is called "All Gold Everything." And, it's about the biggest caricature of black manhood that you've ever seen in your life. Everybody in the video is pretty much running around with guns and money and drugs. Every buffoonish, ignorant, self-destructive stereotype that is fed to our black men on a regular basis is featured in this video. The next book that I'm releasing is related to what I call the gospel of black-male self-destruction, which is being fed to African American males through this music. It's being played out all around us and we see black boys imitating this on a regular basis. It only leads them to either prison or the morgue. We've got to stop it and we've got to deal with it and get it where it stands.

Now, I want to ask you the last question, Dr. Emdin. One of the things that bothered me about Trinidad James is—I would have felt more comfortable if somebody had said,

"Well, you know, he just doesn't know what he does. The poor boy, his IQ is about 80." Which is why his lyrics, as you mentioned, sound like kindergarten nursery rhymes. But, one of the hosts at Power 105 said to me, "You know, he's actually quite articulate and very intelligent." And, I said, "That is a damn shame that an intelligent black man has to be ashamed of his intelligence. He has to hide his intelligence in order to make a dollar." That is pathetic to me.

So, what is your take on that, Dr. Emdin? How deep is this anti-intellectualism issue within commercialized hip-hop; within the broader culture? What is this doing to us as black men?

Dr. Emdin: Well, it's ruining us. I mean... I'll just be completely frank. I've listened to a bunch of Trinidad James' interviews just because I've been curious about this man's psyche. When I initially saw the video and heard the song, I thought the song was catchy. I'm not going to front; when I heard it the first time, I said, "Man, it's a catchy beat." I heard the song and I knew the lyrics were trash and I also watched the video. So, I started researching and listening to interviews. I heard him on 105.1. And, yes, he is articulate. Yes, he can form a sentence. But, the problem is why is it that we should be surprised when a black man can be articulate? Why does it have to be like, "You know what, he actually is." Why can't the stuff that he presents from the beginning be that articulate and that complex self? Why does he have to play a character in order for him to be able to be successful?

But the reality is—my solution and my take on it—and this is not something I've created: There's a bunch of hip-hop scholars and African American scholars that have said this for a very long time. What I'm saying is we've got to reach the point where we start showing people that there is a different narrative. And the piece of that different narrative I'm talking about is that you can have the hypothesized identity. You can rhyme, speak intelligently through that rhyme, be articulate through that rhyme, be aware of politics in your environment through that rhyme and be validated for it. You don't have to be stupid to be accepted. You don't have to play stupid to be accepted. Because, what happens when you're playing a character?

Psychologists tell us this all the time that individuals have core identities and they have role-like identities. The core identity is who you really truly are which expresses your intelligence. Your role identity is the identity that you have to construct in order to be successful in a social stair. If you have a role identity that you enact so consistently, what happens is that it begins to rot your core. You can have a core self and have played a character for so long that you play a game with your mind and you alter your true self by enacting a character for too long. And so, the big problem here is deeper than just this one artist. It's in the fact that this artists creates a narrative that young people start emulating. And the more that they emulate that narrative, it becomes part of their self-construction. It impacts their core identity and starts to rot the intelligence that they have within them—that's the issue.

Dr. Boyce: Wow. That's really deep: life imitating art. Anybody who doesn't believe that the music affects the minds of our kids needs to go to talk to a good psychologist. They will tell you that the repetition of mantra, laced over a smooth continuous repetitive beat, makes your mind open to suggestion and therefore it sinks so deeply into your subconscious that you don't even know it's there. Adolf Hitler said, a long time ago, and people said it before him, that those who control the minds of the people control everything. So when you look at what our kids are absorbing, you can't help but feel that we're in a state of emergency. So, I appreciate you, Dr. Emdin, for stepping on the front line to deal with this issue and to provide that voice that so many of us need. Thank you so much.

Dr. Emdin: Thank you, sir.

Dr. Boyce: Thank you all for checking us out at YourBlackWorld.com. Until we meet again, please, stay strong, be blessed, and be educated.

Spelman College, Keisha Knight-Pulliam and the Death of the Big Booty Hoe

Keshia Knight Pulliam (aka. "Please don't call me Rudy Huxtable") pulled off a massive feat for her alma mater, Spelman College. Pulliam worked with fellow alums and other interested donors to provide a nice financial boost to a school that can always find productive ways to use the money. Keisha and her friends got together to give her school a million dollars to add to its educational war chest, a hefty feat among HBCU alums. Spelman College produces some of the most remarkable and accomplished women I've ever seen, and this kind of greatness doesn't usually happen by accident.

At $284 million dollars, the endowment for Spelman College is more than twice as large as an equally-accomplished school across the street, Morehouse (where I spoke about a month ago). These universities have come to represent the epicenter of African American thought, pride and education. I would gladly send any of my daughters to Spelman, for I truly believe that this is the best university in the nation when it comes to educating African American women.

The neat thing about Pulliam's decision to give back in such a high-profile fashion is that it reminds all of us of the importance of giving to our HBCUs. You don't have to be an HBCU alum in order to give back, since we should be as excited about supporting black students as we are about uplifting black politicians. These young people are our future, and HBCUs hold the key to our educational greatness. Just imagine what would happen if black athletes who earn billions for predominantly white universities took their talents to black schools too.

On a side note, one other thing I love about the ladies of Spelman is the way they stood up to the rapper Nelly, who tried to perform on their campus right after doing a video in which he swiped a credit card in a woman's rear end. Sadly enough, we've gotten to the point where female degradation has become accepted by both men and women, and the days when college aged women protested blatant disrespect by hip-hop artists seems to be a thing of the past. Since that grand moment eight years ago, I've found myself fighting with women on Facebook who think I'm being a lame by asking why Jay-Z was at the Obama campaign event reciting a song with the chorus "I got 99 Problems but a B*tch Ain't One" (he replaced the word "b*tch" with Mitt, but that doesn't escape the fact that he was using the word "b*tch" interchangeably with "woman").

At the same time, my visit to Morehouse was followed by the Rapper 2Chainz, who was also coming to provide some "uplifting insights" for the young black men on campus. I'll admit that, deep down, I fantasize about Spelman women marching across the street to Morehouse College and telling them that it's unacceptable to have 2Chainz coming onto campus to get thousands of black men to recite the chorus: "All I want for my birthday is a big bootie hoe." As any good psychologist will tell you, the recitation of lyrics that convince us to be the very worst of ourselves can sink so deeply into your subconscious that you hardly know that the damage is there.

Rather than searching for "Big booty hoes," I hope Morehouse men will search for big-brained women. They need to look no further than the little Michelle Obamas living right across the street.

Harry Belafonte Calls Out Jay-Z and Beyonce for Selfishness

Harry Belafonte, who did a great deal of work for the black community during the Civil Rights Movement, is making no secret of the fact that he's very disappointed with many young black celebrities when it comes to social activism. Speaking this week with the *Hollywood Reporter*, Belafonte pointed out Jay-Z and Beyonce as prime examples of what he's talking about.

THR: Back to the occasion of the award for your acting career. Are you happy with the image of members of minorities in Hollywood today?

Belafonte: Not at all. They have not told the history of our people, nothing of who we are. We are still looking. We are not determined. We are not driven by some technology that says you can kill Afghanistans, the Iraqis or the Spanish. It is all—excuse my French—s**t. It is sad. And I think one of the great abuses of this modern time is that we should have had such high-profile artists, powerful celebrities. But they have turned their back on social responsibility. That goes for Jay-Z and Beyoncé, for example. Give me Bruce Springsteen, and now you're talking. I really think he is black.

My friend Alexis Stodghill at *TheGrio* makes the point (in a news piece where she carefully cites both sides of the issue) that perhaps Belafonte is off-base with his critique. She notes that Beyonce has spoken up for her fellow recording artist Frank Ocean when he admitted that he was gay, and that Jay-Z has chummed it up with President Obama during his presidential campaign and supported him on the issue of gay marriage.

We must note that Beyonce and Jay-Z speaking up on gay marriage and homosexuality is little more than a political decision designed to remain in alignment with the Obama presidency. If Barack had said nothing on the issue, Jay-Z would have said nothing. So, we have to be sure not to mistake meaningful advocacy for elitist political shoulder-rubbing (wealthy famous people tend to take care of one another).

But when you look at the black aristocracy that is known as Jay-Z and Beyonce, one form of activism that is missing is anything that involves the words "poor black people." Also, when it comes to issues that affect the least of us, including poverty, mass incarceration, urban violence, unequal educational systems and the like, it's easy to say that Jay-Z and Beyonce have been effectively missing in action, unless it's time to show up and utilize this audience to sell albums.

One exception noted by Kirsten West Savali at *NewsOne.com* is the Shawn Carter foundation, created by Jay-Z and the people who work for him. According to the foundation's website, "Since the Foundation's inception, over 750 students have received awards totaling over $1.3 million dollars."

Jay-Z should certainly be commended for doing something he didn't have to do, but let's really think about this for a second, shall we? First, most corporations have some kind of foundation. Even Wal-Mart can claim to have sent thousands of kids to college, as they simultaneously strip workers of their rights around the world, drive small companies out of business and refuse to pay a living wage to their employees.

Secondly, if you divide the $1.3 million given away by the foundation by 750 scholarship recipients, that's about $1,733 per child. Please tell me what college in America has a tuition bill of $1,733. Of course Jay-Z gives away more than most of us can afford, but even the local drug dealer can also afford to use heroin money to give away turkeys at Christmas. The point here is that if I pillage half a billion dollars from the black community over a 10-year period, it's pretty easy for me to give back $1.3 million of it.

I noticed a line in Jay-Z's song "n****z in Paris," where he says, "Can you see the private jets flying over you?" This line is part of a consistent message of black elitism that has become all-too prevalent in the entertainment industry. It is a statement which says, "I'm better than you, and I am not one of you. Your job is to either worship me or hate on me, I don't care which one."

Beyond the "extensive" efforts of his foundation, Jay-Z is also the man who earned over $63 million dollars last year and only gave $6,000 to charity. Unfortunately, this has become par for the course in a world where poor black people are not nearly as fashionable of a cause as gay white kids from the suburbs. Poor black kids can't buy your records, rendering them effectively useless.

So, while Beyonce and Jay-Z speaking up on marriage equality is a politely cute form of activism, you have to agree with Belafonte that today's artists are taught not to care about anyone other than themselves. At best, we might get a photo op at a charity event, but the real pressure to sacrifice for those who are suffering is lost as millions of us forgive celebrities for being unwilling to use their power to make the world a better place. The rule is simple: If you're rich, we love you. It doesn't matter if you're a former crack dealer (Jay-Z), brag about murdering women and children (Lil Wayne) or sleep with middle school kids on the weekends (R. Kelly). Money is used to wash away all sins, and people are quicker to disrespect an icon like Harry Belafonte than they are to challenge celebrities to do more than tweet pictures of their newborn baby.

By "social responsibility," I don't think that Belafonte is referring to charity concerts or speaking to Congress about saving dolphins. He's talking about the kind of activism that requires b***s. He's talking about the black men and women during the 1960s who used their voices loud and clear to state that things need to change in America soon, or else.

Those days are long gone. In the 1960s, oppression was much more rampant, so nearly every black person was banging on the door of equality. Today, those who've been allowed access to predominantly white institutions are asked to sign a "Good negro forever" card, and disavow any meaningful political stands that might get them into trouble with a corporate sponsor or record label. As a result, we have a group of celebrities who are very quick to build their brands off the "street cred" granted to them by impoverished African Americans, but don't feel compelled to use those brands to become anything other than corporate-sponsored slumlords.

So, a "gangsta rapper" can speak all day about his time in prison, but he dare not say anything about the fact that the United States incarcerates more of its citizens than any country in the world, earning billions on the backs of black men and women, destroying millions of families in the process. He can rap all about "all his homies that done passed away," but he's better off staying away from a conversation about how gun violence is fueled by manufacturers who are happy to build profitable corporate tools to fund black male genocide.

It is the lack of acknowledgement of the deep and piercing artifacts of black oppression that bother Belafonte and others the most. It's what bothers me too, for I've always been raised to believe that (to recite the words of

Spiderman's Uncle Ben) *great power comes with great responsibility.*

Perhaps when Jay-Z really understands what wealth is all about, he can take a note from Warren Buffett, Oprah and others, who've convinced several billionaires to give half of their wealth to charity when they die. A billion dollars is far more than enough for one family so why not use the rest of save 1,000 families? Is it nothing less than utterly shameful to have 10 houses, 15 cars, 200 expensive suits and several private planes? Maybe there is a point where such gluttony should not be celebrated by the rest of us, and instead be called out as pathetic in a world where millions of children are going to die this year from starvation.

Anyone who disagrees with me might want to consider the fact that there is nothing consistent with the teachings of Jesus about letting innocent people starve while you're burning money in your basement. The principled embraced by men like Muhammad Ali, who gave away nearly everything to stand up for his values, are virtually non-existence when our leading artists write songs about excessive materialism, getting high and drunk every day, killing other black men and unhealthy s****l promiscuity.

Belafonte is right on point and we should look to our elders to remind us of what it means to live a purposeful and righteous life.

Harry Belafonte, by speaking up at the age of 85, is effectively asking that young people pick up the baton that he's been running since Dr. King was a teenager. But instead of picking up the baton, we've thrown it at his feet and signed ourselves up for corporate slavery. I congratulate Harry for taking a stand on this important issue, and I am hopeful that his courage can spark the cultural revolution necessary to make our people stronger as a result.

Way to go Harry, I respect you.

Hip Hop Artists Must Start Giving Back to the Black Community

Uncle Luke from 2 Live Crew put hip hop artists on blast for not standing up for their communities while they seem glad to drain all available resources. Speaking to the Miami New Times, Luke issued this ultimatum:

"I've got a message for Lil Wayne, his Cash Money Brothers, DJ Khaled, Puff Daddy and all the rappers from other parts of the country who now live in Miami," he said. "I'm tired of seeing these cats using up our beaches, soaking up our sunshine, taking over the nightclubs, and sleeping with our women without investing anything into the community."

Luke continued to rail on his fellow artists about their lack of interest in supporting the people who give them so much.

"I want to know when Lil Wayne is going to do more than show up courtside at the American Airlines Arena" Luke continued. "H-ll, it's not like he paid for them anyway. You know he got comped. This free loading and mooching of my city has got to stop. There used to be a day when out of town rappers were scared to throw their weight around

Miami. It didn't matter if they were coming from New York or Los Angeles, they knew better than to act like they owned this mother f--ker."

Luke continued on with his interesting statement:

> "I'm giving them a deadline" Luke said. "They got until January 1. If I don't see them giving back to the Magic City, I'm gonna have their Miami cards revoked. They won't be getting into any more nightclubs. They won't be able to go near our women. And Lil Wayne is gonna have to find floor seats for New Orleans Hornets home games because he won't be allowed inside the Triple A."

While I find it a bit odd that Luke talks about "sleeping with our women" as if they are possessions, I get his broader point. The artist seems to be referring to the fact that the hip hop industry has lost its soul when it comes to using its power to achieve meaningful social change for the millions of Americans who support the industry. While there is no shortage of rappers willing to brag about how many friends they've seen go to jail, very few of them are willing to talk about the ills of mass incarceration that have served to destroy the Black family in America.

I hear artists rap about friends who've been shot in the street, but there is little serious political conversation about gun control. This doesn't even begin to touch the toxic message of self-destruction that too many artists have come to embrace as a form of psychological genocide that continues to undermine the potential of an entire generation. I long for the days when Black men encourage one another to be well-educated and hardworking, and chastise one another for being lazy and irresponsible.

But in too many situations, the latter is applauded, while all forms of intellectual achievement end up being murdered in broad daylight.

Luke's remarks are a relevant wake up call to the sleeping giants within hip hop. Artists should be called to action to help deal with the problems that affect all of Black America, not just Miami. It's not only a matter of giving money or making quick appearances. Hip hop artists should form coalitions to achieve social progress that are similar to those that exist in Hollywood. We must grow beyond thinking that having money in your bank account somehow makes your existence worthwhile. There is nothing fulfilling about spending your time running from one party to another—it's actually kind of empty and pathetic.

So, good job Uncle Luke. I've honestly never liked the man's music, but I appreciate at least a piece of his vision. I doubt that his challenge to other artists is going to get a positive response (since beef and 'ignant' stuff sells records), but I hope that the people of his city back his sentiments. To whom much is given, much is expected. Hip hop artists get everything from their people, and it is now time that they return the favor.

Jay-Z Isn't a Bad Role Model for Black Business, But There are Others Too

Jay-Z is an amazing rapper. Some think that he's been in the game for a bit too long, but I don't agree. Personally, I think "Jigga" simply reflects the fact that hip-hop itself is aging. Jazz was once solely the domain of rebellious teenagers, but now you're sure to hear it playing in every old folk's home across America. The same is going to be true for hip-hop.

Jay-Z has said repeatedly that he will stop making music, and I'm sure that one day he will. However, there is one area in which we need to retire Jay-Z: In his role as the pre-eminent black businessman in America. It's not that Jay-Z is a bad role model, it's just that he's been exhausted.

Don't get me wrong, Jigga has made significant amounts of money by busting rhymes on his left and selling clothes on his right. Good for him. But is he really the best business role model for young black males, who are already consumed with a culture that teaches them that all they can be are rappers or athletes? No, he is not. Young black women also find that their leading role models in business are women like Oprah and Beyonce, both of whom keep us hyper-fixated on the entertainment industry. It's time to make a change.

When our kids are looking for business role models, why not consider people like Dr. Randal Pinkett (The Apprentice), Ursula Burns (CEO of Xerox), Ken Chenault (CEO of American Express), or Chuck Creekmur (founder of AllHipHop.com). These individuals are educated self-starters who used a variety of brilliant and creative methods to either get to the top of the corporate ladder or to build their own corporate ladders. Sure, some of them are linked to entertainment, but they are the bosses of the industry and not one of the slaves.

Black males especially would gain from having a new set of role models to encourage us to more effectively target our collective genius. Many of us only dream of throwing footballs and dribbling basketballs, leaving education on the table for others to use against us. Rather than finding the real money and opportunity that comes from being the smartest guy in the room, we are deliberately choosing to be the dumb jock with a fifth grade reading level. This should be unacceptable for us all.

Jay-Z and others like him are tremendous beneficiaries of media. Media tends to focus on the most glamorous and entertaining African Americans, rather than the most impactful. Women like Fantasia were sucked into thinking that the decisions to drop out of school and to become a teen parent would all be corrected by one lucky stop at the *American Idol* audition. Not only did most of us see the destruction of Fantasia's dream, we also see the millions of other Fantasia wannabes who gave up everything to live the high life of entertainment, but got the welfare office instead.

It's a new century, so black folks need a new paradigm. The former entertainer or athlete who becomes a successful businessperson is certainly worthy of our respect. But few success stories in black America run through Hollywood, the recording studio or the NBA. Instead, the greatest and most powerful success stories in black America run through the classroom. Let's make sure our kids don't forget that.

Dr. Boyce: Does Michelle Obama Want Her Daughters to Be Like Beyonce?

A lot of conversation has centered around the growing love affair between first lady Michelle Obama and Beyonce Knowles. Beyonce sent Michelle a very nice public letter, sharing her admiration for the first lady. Michelle responded by tweeting "Thank you for the beautiful letter and for being a role model who kids everywhere can look up to."

Perhaps in the spirit of hip-hop, I should have (as Reilly on "The Boondocks" would) said the words "pause" and "no h**o" before discussing how close these two women have become.

But out of respect for President Obama's announcement in support of gay marriage, I would like to publicly banish the term "no h**o" from my vocabulary.

With that being said, eyebrows were extra arched as one amazing first lady (Michelle) has become especially chummy with a first lady in her own right (Beyonce). One woman is married to the leader of the free world, and the other is married to the world's most famous slum lord (did I say that?). OK, Jay-Z isn't a slum lord, but he is a very talented artist who goes around the world calling himself a "Ni**a in Paris," where he even refers to Beyonce as the "b*tch in his home." When I get married, I don't expect that my wife will be happy to hear that I've called her a b*tch in public, no matter how much money some white guy paid me to say it.

But in spite of their superstar husbands, neither of these women are *Basketball Wives*, whose greatest source of achievement comes from the hard work of someone else. Beyonce has earned more than her husband Jay-Z, and Michelle would probably make a better president than Barack (well, she would at least be a better black president).

Both women are beautiful and intelligent wives, mothers, and career women. That point is abundantly clear.

Some wonder, however, if Beyonce is an adequate role model for young women. My friend Demetria Lucas at *TheRoot.com* openly questioned whether or not Michelle should be following Beyonce around the country and sending tweets of admiration across cyberspace. I can understand where Demetria is coming from, since we can say that Beyonce did choose to marry a former drug dealer and made a song (Soldier) encouraging young girls to date dudes with "hood status" who "carry big thangs," "make money three ways," and "keep it real." That song irked me to no end because a whole lot of brothers have died or gone to prison trying to "keep it real" over some nonsense.

But as we think about what Beyonce represents, the good clearly outweighs the bad. She carries herself with a tremendous amount of grace, poise and civility that makes her worthy of her superstar status. She's not like Rihanna, seen on a blog every week smoking weed with no top on. She's not beating women down on television like Evelyn Lozada, and she's living her life with dignity in a media space that loves to see black women at their absolute worst.

Is Beyonce a bad role model for black women? I don't think so. The mutual respect between Michelle, Oprah Winfrey and Beyonce represents growing empowerment among women in a country where women now officially comprise the majority of the American workforce. Michelle and Beyonce are not feminists, they are womanists. They are proud to be feminine, accept some traditional gender roles, but command the respect that they deserve. They know they don't need a man, but they allow themselves to need good men in order to make their relationships work and that makes them both powerful and lovable, which is an awesome combination.

I don't think that Michelle wants Sasha and Malia to grow up and marry their own version of Jay-Z (if Malia's boyfriend ever calls her a b*tch, he might end up in Guantanamo Bay). But, there are a few things that they can learn from their mother's friends, all of whom show them a little bit of what it means to be an empowered black woman in America. That sounds pretty good to me.

Dr. Boyce: Katt Williams Reflects the Breakdown of Black Men Everywhere

Watching the life of Katt Williams is like watching a plane crash in slow motion, the kind of crash where the pilot tells you that you're going down 20 minutes before you're actually dead. The slow decay of one of the great comedians of our time is painful to watch, since we saw another great comedian by the name of Richard Pryor go through the same thing 30 years ago.

I don't presume to know why Katt engages in one form of odd behavior after another, but I do know he loves bragging about getting high all the time. In fact, the brother seems to get arrested more often than President Obama appears on television, and many of his antics are indicative of drug use, mental illness or both. Sadly, it appears that Katt's extraordinary genius and all that he's worked for are going right down the drain, and he honestly doesn't seem to care.

When I watch Katt make one faulty personal decision after another, I think about my older brother who died just six months ago. He wasn't technically my older brother (he was a young uncle), but like a lot of black families, definitions of relatives are, well, relative. He was eight years older than me and I looked up to him the way a stump looks up to an Oak tree. I followed him around for the bulk of my young life, and spent quite a few years hoping that he was the man that I wanted him to be, instead of the man that he actually was.

Like Katt, my brother also seemed to love drugs and alcohol. In fact, I give him credit for my decision to never touch either one, since his life taught me everything that I did NOT want to do in order to be successful. His demise was inevitable, just like Katt's, and it was equally difficult to watch. Various addictions, compounded with a few stints in jail and prison, facilitated various forms of mental illness that made him socially, physically, spiritually and psychologically impotent. During his last three years, as he laid paralyzed in the hospital, I saw this as a fitting end to a life full of disappointment. By that time, I'd taken the role of the older brother, and when I reflect on his life, I can't remember too many good times.

Both Katt and my brother's experience, along with countless others being recalled by people reading this article, should remind us of the dangers of excessive drug and alcohol consumption in the African American community. Nearly every hip-hop artist put on the radio by some big, money hungry, racist corporation wants you to believe that every black man in America wants to stay high and drunk, popping bottles at the club every Friday night. Did you ever notice that commercialized hip-hop is the only genre of music that speaks consistently about the same things in nearly every single song?

Here's a newsflash: Nothing great has ever been achieved by a group of people who spent all their time getting high and drunk every day. Part of the reason that others are glad to see black men sprinting toward the drug dealer and liquor bottle is because they know that if we are obsessed with obtaining the next high, then we won't be competing for PhDs, JDs and multi-million dollar contracts. Kall Williams is a perfect case-in point, since his antics are going to end up costing him and his family at least $10 million dollars over the course of his career.

So, here's the point: Maybe it's OK to tell our boys to avoid drugs and alcohol all together. Sure, some of them aren't going to listen, but a positive message must be pushed in order to counter all of the destructive imagery that's being fed to our boys on a daily basis. In my own feeble effort to turn a negative into a positive, my brother was the reason I created the Building Outstanding Men and Boys Family

Empowerment Series, to talk about principles that our boys must learn in order to survive in a world that is designed to kill them. The reality is that if we don't teach good principles to young men, then they have little chance of growing into adequate husbands and fathers.

When I met with Min. Louis Farrakhan last week, he and I were both in agreement that it is not a coincidence that destructive music with a toxic message has taken over the airwaves of most black communities across America: A black man with a bottle in his hand is not nearly as intimidating as a black man holding a book. The first man seeks to perpetuate racist institutions, and the second one might be enlightened enough to fight them. By speaking honestly about the dangers of drugs and alcohol in our society, we can protect our sons, save ourselves and elevate our community. This nonsense must be confronted by us all.

Tyra Banks to Play Life-Size Doll for Little White Girl, Just Like Richard Pryor

"Loving yourself is paramount, no matter what shape, size or color you are. I call it being flawsome: you + your flaws + awesome = flawsome." These are the words from the great Tyra Banks, who is set to grace the cover of Cosmopolitan South Africa next month. Tyra is an awesome role model for almost any young woman, since she preaches that beauty must be accompanied by brains and high self-esteem to make our girls successful.

Variety is reporting that Tyra is going to star in a sequel to the made-for-TV film, "Life Size." Banks appeared with Lindsay Lohan in the film back in 2000. We doubt that Lindsay is going to be in this one, since she is too busy being arrested. The film involves Banks coming to life as a massive doll for Lohan, after the little girl tries to use voodoo to bring her mom back to life.

Doesn't this remind you of the Richard Pryor classic, "The Toy?" In case you're not old enough to remember this classic film, "The Toy" was yet another case in which a black person was presented to the audience as a play thing for a little white child. Of course, the black character always brings "spice" to the household, the same way nannies did on old southern plantations 150 years ago. For some reason, having the large Negro sidekick is a lasting tradition in Hollywood.

I'm not one to say that Tyra shouldn't take the role, since I expect she's being well-compensated for it. But I have to admit that I'm not all that comfortable with white kids using black people as toys, dolls, cartoon characters or hand puppets. I also wonder if these films would be as entertaining or successful if a white person were playing the sidekick to a black child. Kind of tough to picture that one, isn't it?

Of course these thoughts are not meant to demean Tyra in any way; she'll always be among my top ten most beautiful women on the planet (behind my mother, grandmother, daughters, sister, and girlfriend, of course). But maybe these roles give us something to think about and also teach us about ourselves as a racially-damaged country. Portraying black people as caricatures hardly presents America as a post-racial society.

TJ Holmes Speaks Candidly about BET, The Psychological Drug Dealers of America

This week, TJ Holmes, host of the new BET show "Don't Sleep!" took a trip to Power 105.1 in New York City to speak about his new show and the challenges of developing a new audience. Charlamagne Tha God, one of the hosts of the show ("The Breakfast Club"), sent me a copy of the interview (which you can see below), for he shares my concern with what BET has chosen to become.

I've respected Charlamagne since I met him in 2006 when I appeared a few times on the Wendy Williams Experience. He treated me with tremendous decency long before anyone knew or cared who I was. He's also an honest advocate for the challenges of the black male in America which makes him an important ally in the struggle for black liberation and advancement.

I watched the interview curiously, impressed by the honesty with which Holmes went about sharing his challenges with the new show, and how his network is both supporting him and fighting with him. His courageous decision to speak so honestly about the difficulty of developing quality content and a good audience for BET gives an inside look at how hard it can be to rise from the gutter once you've become committed to making it into your home. Sadly enough, BET has defined itself to be the White Trash of Black America, appealing to the worst in us, lowering IQs and killing dreams like a KKK firing squad in front of the house of Malcolm X.

Someone needs to take on BET, and it needs to be all of us. BET is owned by people who care almost nothing for our community, for their only goal is to maximize the bottom line. The problem is that it's difficult for TJ Holmes to compete with Lil Wayne, 2 Chainz (author of the song with the brilliant chorus, "All I want for my birthday is a big booty hoe") or any other form of buffoonery the network could be putting on the air. So, the good folks at both BET and Viacom (their economic plantation owners) must be compelled to consider a double bottom line, where they are reminded of the value of inspiring young black people with positive role models and a reclamation of black intellectualism on mainstream TV.

BET is the psychological drug dealer, standing on the corner, "clocking the dough," with the "Big booty hoe" in the front seat of his Mercedes. He may not be bothering you, but he's got his eye on your children when they get out of school. He's showing them flashy cars and handfuls of money to convince them to skip college so they can become drug dealers or drug addicts. Largely due to the existence of BET, we've got an entire generation of black youth who've become addicted to the drug of counterproductive buffoonery, and TJ Holmes is part of the rehabilitation process. If BET really wants to improve, they need to let this brother breathe.

Even Adolph Hitler understood that he who controls the media, also controls the mind. So Hitler would surely be applauding the achievements of BET, for the network has contributed to black psychological and actual genocide through the rejection of education, increased drug/alcohol consumption, higher HIV rates and the glorification of handgun violence among young black men. Even BET founder Sheila Johnson has admitted that the network has played a role in harming our children, so if we love our children, we will fight to the death to protect their well-being. In black America, we must go to the corner and kill, incarcerate or control our psychological drug dealers. If we do not, our community's demise is imminent.

Dr. Boyce: BET, When It Comes to TJ Holmes, Either Grow Up or Give Up

I've done a lot of work with various media outlets over the years, but it has left me relatively unsatisfied. The reason for my concern is that, as a business school professor, I tend to notice ownership structure, incentives and the role that capitalist organizations have played in the oppression and control of black people. Like infants being fed Vodka in their baby bottles, black people are consistently doused with an overwhelming amount of unhealthy propaganda, leading many of us to live our lives as the intellectual version of the walking dead.

There is no network that embodies this problematic disparity more than Black Entertainment Television (BET). I love BET for what it could have been, but I hate the network for what it chooses to be. BET has become a case study for all that can go wrong from a one-dimensional focus on corporate profitability with almost no concern for the externalities being created by destructive and irresponsible content. Even worse is that BET is ultimately run and controlled by Viacom, a company headed by executives who don't have to go home to gun violence, sagging pants, educational underachievement and all the other cultural deformities that come from consuming weaponized psychological poison for the entire day.

One ray of hope for BET was the new show, "Don't Sleep!" hosted by TJ Holmes. Almost no new show in the history of BET has generated as much buzz in the black community, at least among those with more than a 10th-grade reading level. Like the drunk a*s uncle who suddenly decides that he wants to take care of his kids, BET claimed that it was trying to turn over a new leaf and give us something that makes the black community better and not worse.

The problem for BET, similar to the uncle who suddenly decides to be a father, is the lack of trust. The network has abused our brains with the kind of garbage that could serve as a How-to Guide for the Willie Lynch syndrome and produced its content with almost no degree of corporate accountability. I even remember watching the rapper Wiz Khalifa perform a song ("On my Level") where he bragged to an audience full of teenagers about "being sloppy drunk looking for the keys to my car."

Most of us turned off BET years ago and can't even find it on our cable guide. Like the ex-girlfriend who slept with your best friend and stole your money, most of us feel that we escaped from the BET psychological plantation and can't quite stomach the idea of coming back. But TJ's show seemed different and special.

Holmes took his powerful brand away from the lilly white safe havens of CNN and brought it back to his community. Many of us hearing about the amazing guests and quality conversations on the show were saying, "I think I'm going to take a look." The trust was coming back, and people were ready to take notice.

But before you could say the words, "I heart coonery," BET cut TJ's show back from five half-hour days a week to just one day per week (extending the show to one hour), simultaneously attempting to argue that the change means that they are giving TJ more time on the air instead of less. Sorry BET, but most of us know that five and a half hours per week is more than one. This is something we learned when we chose to pick up a math book instead of watching 106 & Park.

So, BET allows for a show that significantly changes the direction of the network, the host does a great job, the show has solid ratings in spite of mediocre lead-ins and they kill it in just a month? The problem here is that the network should have at least given TJ three months on his original schedule to build an audience for the show instead of expecting him to overcome thirty years of misdirection in just a month. If I didn't know any better, I'd think that this show was actually set up for failure.

I respect BET President Debra Lee, but I have to be honest. Rather than assuming responsibility for taking the show off the air, the network heads will likely lay the blame into the hands of black people themselves. I can hear Debra saying, "See, we tried to offer you Negroes something positive, but you refused to watch it." Such a statement would be made without regard to the fact that most of the quality audience left BET a long time ago, and it's going to take some time and money to get them back. But an exceedingly materialistic corporate model h**l bent against the idea of delayed gratification is likely not going to make the kind of investment necessary to clean up a mess that began back when Michael Jackson was still a young s*x symbol.

Sorry Debra, but you and I both know that you can't blame black people for this one. You never gave this show a chance, you never gave it adequate marketing and you never gave TJ the support that your network would gladly give to a baby killing gangster like Lil Wayne. You can't feed a child cookies and grease every day for 20 years and then expect him to lose weight with one day of exercise. Similarly, you can't build a multi-billion dollar network on a perpetual dose of psychological poison and then expect your audience to suddenly become enlightened.

TJ Holmes is good for BET, and I hope that Debra Lee understands that. But if the lives of Martin Luther King, Gandhi and even Jesus show us, you are usually going to be crucified for trying to do the right thing. Anyone trying to save BET might just be wasting their time, for almost none of its leaders has the courage to push for something different. In order to make progress, you must be willing to embrace the struggle necessary in order to move forward. If you say you want something better, but aren't fully prepared to make that investment, then your actions have told us everything we need to know.

Star Jones Drops The Ball On 'Basketball Wives'

Star Jones is interesting. She's smart, crafty and typically quite classy, but I admittedly cocked my head to the side like Scooby-Doo, when I read that Jones said that she never intended to boycott the show *Basketball Wives*. Speaking to another woman, Wendy Williams, who I appreciate dearly, Star said, "I was never encouraging anybody to boycott somebody's job. That's not what I'm about."

Star's words are a far cry from her previous tweets on the matter, where she took a far more militant point of view: "It may be 'comfortable' to be quiet when women of color slap the crap out of each other & run across tables barefoot, but #ENOUGHisENOUGH," she tweeted. "About to put together a group of sisters to finally 'tell the truth' about the image of women of color in the media."

"And the thought that the woman from #BBW who was smacked doesn't have the RIGHT to file assault charges is LUDICROUS," she said. "You NEVER give up your right not to have your 'person' intentionally assaulted unless you are participating in an agreed physical activity. I'm asking all my high profile, platform having conscientious sisters who

STAND FOR SOMETHING to just say #ENOUGHisENOUGH & call folk out! Be mad. But think about what I said. WE ARE BETTER than that. You're either part of the problem or part of the solution."

Perhaps the Star Jones from last month should be introduced to the Star Jones from this month because they appear to be different people.

I've rarely, if ever, seen anyone back pedal this fast when it comes to taking a stand on such an important issue. I wouldn't doubt that this has a lot to do with money, since Star herself is a reality TV star, but it certainly goes to show how money and fame can modify our point of view.

My perspective is that Star Jones may be doing a "shake down" of VH1 and its producers. In other words, I wouldn't be surprised to see her on the next season of "Basketball Wives," perhaps as a contributor whose job it is to convince the women to stop fighting so much, kind of like a referee at a boxing match or trainer at the zoo. It's hard to imagine how the world is better off with Star becoming buddies with Evelyn Lozada, the Chief Assault Artist for the show. So in some ways, Star may have made herself part of the problem, not the solution.

Star needs VH1 and VH1 may need Star (to stop criticizing their show). For example, the ratings for *Basketball Wives* have been in constant decline. There is a long list of corporate sponsors running for the hills, indicating that the show's producers are nervous. This is further shown by the fact that many of its leading lady gangstas (namely Evelyn Lozada and Tami Roman) are having a series of highly publicized "coming-to-Jesus" moments, where they want you to understand that it was childhood trauma that makes them want to bash in the face of the woman next to them.

Star Jones, thanks for at least getting the rest of us riled up, even if you yourself are now sinking back into the comfort of the establishment.

For those who still care about protecting young girls from being taught to bully one another, the fight must go on. There are thousands of young women all across America who are suicidal or traumatized due to the "little Evelyns" sprouting up all across the country, and its up to the adults around them to stand up and protect these kids.

The key to dealing with a bully is coming together and fighting to the end. We cannot allow "Basketball Wives" to bully the rest of us into submission. For a variety of economic reasons, the premise of the show will probably never change. Therefore, the only solution is to get rid of the show entirely.

Dr. Boyce: Coonery 101 – 10 Things I Need to be a Rapper on the Radio

It's hard for me to critique the monstrosity that has become commercialized hip-hop culture. I love hip hop and didn't even start listening to music until hip-hop hit the scene. I am a serious fan of quite a few artists, both young and old. However, hip-hop (at least the stuff we hear on the radio) calls for an intervention, like the relative you love who has been hitting the crack pipe for way too long. The intervention is necessary to protect our kids from receiving poisonous messages that are wired to ruin their lives.

One of the things that drives me crazy about commercialized hip-hop is that the art form has lost the bulk of its creativity.

When I listen to white guys on the radio, they sing about all kinds of stuff: the birds in the sky, the iPod they just bought, the girl they are trying to go out on a date with, their days in high school, etc. Brothers don't have that kind of range: We're only allowed to rap about the same tired stuff that the other dude rapped about in the last song. "Imma spend it on ya shawty, bottles of Patron fo ya shawty, got my gun for the haters, diamonds on my neck, I'm a playa"...blah, blah, blah, whatever man.

So, to make my point, I thought I would lay out the 10 things that any person needs in order to be a rapper, at least the kind of rapper who gets on the radio. Call it the Creative c**n Instant Rapper Fun Kit. I'm sure that every white boy in Iowa already has one:

1) **A really large and overpriced piece of jewelry that you borrowed money to buy:** It can have diamonds, gold, platinum, or whatever and has to be really heavy, as if it might crush your testicles if you move too fast. Oh, why is your favorite jeweler snickering at you and calling you in the middle of the night to tell you about another piece he just made? Because he knows you're gonna be broke after your next album drops and wants to milk your dumb a** before it's too late.

2) **Your body must be tattooed so much that even your mama doesn't recognize you:** I'm just waiting for a rapper to tattoo his own eyeballs, now that would be gangsta. You better keep making hit records, because it's hard to get a job with tattoos all over your neck, just ask Thugnificent from the Boondocks.

3) **You have to be drinking out of a bottle of something that is eventually going to kill you:** If you are going to be a real rapper, liquor must become a food group. You know
Uncle Joe, the alcoholic who lives in yo grandma's basement? He used to act just like you 20 years ago.

4) **A gun so you can blast all haters on sight (The Haterologist Extermination Program):** You're only keeping it real if you shoot another black man, white boys don't count. You can even sell more records if you rap about it, especially if you went to prison. As black men, we can officially say, that we've killed more black people than the KKK. (Oh snap, did that rhyme? Now dats wussup!)

5) **A whole lot of gold, diamonds and other random jewelry in your mouth:** You should be setting off metal detectors, even when you're b**t-naked.

6) **A pack of random women around you, preferably strippers, all of whom you slept with last night:** Don't worry about the fact that they've had s*x with hundreds of dudes before you. AIDS only happens to other people, Eazy-E was a fluke.

7) **A pound of weed, an ounce of coke, or a bottle of 'Sizzurp' somewhere in the vicinity:** There's nothing more productive than a black man who is so high that he can't even get out of bed in the morning. That was Dr. King's dream, Malcolm's too.

8) **A gang of dudes who follow you everywhere you go for no particular reason:** You're not a real rapper without a bunch of straight-up thugs from your childhood who are there to "protect" you, but end up shooting somebody at a club who then sues you for everything you've got.

9) **A pocket full of cash so you can make it rain at the club:** Don't save or invest your money, that's actin white. Just go to the club and throw money in the air and take pictures on Twitter with hundred dollar bills hanging out of your hat, that's what Bill Gates and Oprah do with their money too.

10) **A full-fledge plan of weaponized, mass-marketed self-destruction:** By being determined to reflect only the worst and most ruinous parts of your humanity, you have become a virus to your community

and an exaggerated caricature, thus creating a modern day minstrel show. Your over-the-top behavior is a reflection of the crabs-in-a-barrel mindset of impoverished, uneducated black men competing for attention by showing that their urban experience is more authentic than the next dude. You are exporting a false version of the "hood experience" to those who believe that the trauma of urban America is exciting, fun and intriguing, like watching elephants mate in the middle of the jungle.

Every little boy who looks up to you and emulates your distorted perception of manhood and blackness is walking right off a cliff that lands him in a casket, the poorhouse, or a prison cell. You, and the multi-billion dollar plantation owner who keeps you high, ignorant and unfocused, are destroying the futures of millions of kids who ignore their parents and pay attention to you. When you consider the death toll of black men in America, one can easily argue that you're part of an extermination plan no less deadly than what Hitler did during World War II.

BET's President Explains Why She Doesn't Offer More Positive Programming

Last fall, BET's President, Debra Lee, commented on the style of programming being offered by her network and the response from her viewers. At the same time, Sheila Johnson, co-founder of BET, criticized the network for its offerings, stating that the company squandered a chance to give black America a voice. Lee and Johnson's remarks open the door for an intriguing dialogue about the power of media to shape minds, and whether or not we've been using this power responsibly.

In an article on *TheRoot.com*, Sheryl Huggins Solomon asked if black people really want to have a voice at all. Her measuring stick of whether or not we want that voice appears to be related to our decision to watch the BET show hosted by TJ Holmes, "Don't Sleep!" I became immediately concerned with Sheryl's column because it seemed to argue that it's the audience's fault that BET has become determined to produce toxic programming. Also, the idea of daring black people to support your event in order to prove their blackness is not much different from what Tavis Smiley did to President Obama back when he called him out for not attending his "State of the Black Union" event back in 2008.

At a screening for a new BET documentary, someone asked Lee if the network was going to aim for better programming, with Lee stating that, "Over the 28 years I've been at BET, we've tried different shows, series and nightly news, and it's always a matter of what are people going to show up to watch. We started a new show last week called Don't Sleep! With T.J. Holmes, which is supposed to address these kinds of issues. It's designed to be a mix of entertainment and news and commentary. We hoped it would have been a Jon Stewart, Stephen Colbert-type show."

Lee then went on to explain that the ratings game is what drives her to continue with content that is less than desirable:

> "To be honest, the ratings haven't been great in the past two weeks (referring to Holmes' show). Our audience always says they want this kind of programming, but they don't show up," Lee said.

Here's the challenge for Debra Lee. First, when you consider the impact that positive programming is going to have on your audience, you have to realize what kind of audience you've created. I can't tell you how many educated black folks I've met who simply say, "I refuse to watch BET anymore." So, effectively, a disproportionate chunk of the BET audience might consist of people who either enjoy brain dead programming or only look to BET to give them brain dead programming. You can't give your child candy for breakfast, lunch and dinner until he's 10 years old, and then expect him to become a Vegan.

The second problem for BET (which I discuss in more detail in my book, "Black American Money") is capitalism. As a Finance Professor, I teach on Capitalism all the time. As a black man, I've noted how our addiction to hardcore capitalism has made it nearly impossible for African Americans to achieve liberation as a people. Raw capitalism effectively convinces you that money is the most important thing in the world—or, as a rapper on BET might say, "If it don't make dolluhs shawty, then it don't make sense." The easiest path to slavery is to form an addiction to a commodity that you do not control.

The problem with the "Money Rules" methodology is that it doesn't make much room for a double bottom line that also incorporates social responsibility as part of your business model. So, if TJ Holmes gets a million viewers and Lil Wayne gets 1.5 million, capitalism tells you to drop TJ so you can show more of Weezy. What this model fails to consider is that the creation of more toxic programming further undermines the intellectual quality of your audience, making it even more difficult for the next TJ Holmes to have a successful show. This also fails to mention the negative externalities produced by teaching a million black kids to act like Lil Wayne.

My advice to Debra Lee? Make your money, but allow the garbage to subsidize the intellectual health food. TJ's show might not make as much money as the BET Awards, but he is an intelligent black man, a great role model, and someone with the capacity to bring positive issues to light for a struggling community. The fat child who's been given candy his whole life might not like the vegetables at first, but if you throw in a bit of health food with the fattening stuff, he might actually learn to appreciate it. Remember: Billionaire Bob Johnson could have still made several hundred million dollars by creating more conscientious programming. I don't fault the brother for making money; instead, I fault him for WORSHIPPING money at the expense of his own community.

Again, I'm a Finance professor, so I understand the value and power of a dollar bill.

BET's audience is a reflection of what the network has become over the years, and with the democratization of media, they've lost some of their relevance. To regain a quality audience that appreciates quality programming, we can't just rely on money-hungry, myopic investments that only allow you to consider the next quarter's profit margin. But the challenge for BET is that when white people own you, your latitude for creating positive black programming is severely diminished, since the white executive in the suburbs could care less if the network he runs is teaching black boys to murder one another in the street. This, my friends, is why we must have more black-owned, conscientious media, for the only way to true freedom is to learn how to control our own public imagery.

Russell Simmons Defends Gwyneth's Use of the N-Word....Don't Do it Man

I recently read an article in which Russell Simmons defended Gwyneth Paltrow in her use of the word "n*gga" to define her time in Paris with Jay-Z, Beyonce and the rest of her "n*ggas." Gwyneth, like most "down-ass" white girls who get very comfortable around black folks, caught herself slipping into territory that only the bravest white people go.

I stand with Russell in that Gwyneth is not entirely to blame. At worst, we can blame Gwyneth for not being sensitive enough to realize that Jay-Z and Kanye are not ambassadors of the black community who've been given creative license to sell and market the word n*gga to audiences around the world. Most of us aren't getting any of the royalties being paid to Kanye and Jay-Z from their decision to sell out.

Now, back to Russell, Gwyneth, Jigga, and N*gga. Russell, a man who has far more money than I'll ever have, went out of his way to defend Jay-Z and Kanye as "poets" who deserve the creative freedom to express themselves in ways that they see fit. I find it interesting that black self-respect must be consistently sacrificed for the sake of creative freedom. I have to openly wonder if the Asian community would be happy to hear about "Chinks in Paris," or if Jews would support a song called "Hymies in Paris." In fact, I doubt that Russell could ever release such an album without having his power ripped out from under him.

Says Russell:

> 'I have NEVER told any artist not to use that word or any word in my life and I never will; a poet can choose their own words to describe whatever they want in their art."

Mind you, Russell's careful selection of words like "art" and 'poet" are wired to pre-empt the inevitable battleground that emerges when we realize that the minds of millions of black children are being destroyed, all so a bunch of grown men can have access to their precious art. The difficult reality that Russell and other proud "n*ggas" in commercialized hip-hop must face is the fact that their music does little to elevate the masses, and only serves to make black boys think that it's cool to stay high and drunk, have sex with everything that moves, kill each other on the street, disrespect black women and waste their money popping bottles at the club.

Of course, little Paquan in the hood doesn't have to choose Jay-Z and Kanye as his role models, but since all of his friends at school are influenced by the artists they hear on the radio every single day, he is constantly bombarded with messages that serve as a personal blueprint to his own self-destruction (get the joke? Notice that I used the word "blueprint").

So, in the quest to protect the rights of "poets" to pursue their "art," we are promoting the very worst that the black community has to offer. Toxic thinking and behavior is being packaged and exported to predominantly white audiences around the world so that individuals like Russell Simmons and Jay-Z can get rich. As a result of this deformed re-branding of the black community, white women like Gwyneth Paltrow think that we are all a pack of n*ggas who want to hang out with her in Paris. In fact, being a n*gga has become so cool that Gwyneth wants to be a n*gga too.

Let's be clear: Much of the commercialized hip-hop that we hear on the radio cannot be readily defended as art. The core of the artistic value of music is undermined when a music industry executive walks in the room and says, "Kanye, don't rap about Jesus or living in the suburbs. Just call yourself a n*gga and refer to black women as b*tches. That's how you can sell more records." It is at that point that the so-called "art" being produced in the studio turns into nothing more than a corporate commodity being sold to those who love seeing black people put on monkey minstrel shows. The mouth full of gold teeth, tattoos up your neck and ten gold chains are nothing short of comedic exaggerations of the black male as a hyper-aggressive animal who will eat and murder other black men on sight.

The bottom line is that commercialized hip-hop is not producing artists. It is actually producing a whole pack of n*ggas. So, with all due respect to anyone who wants to sit here and pretend that it's OK for white people to refer to the black people around them as n*ggas, perhaps it's time to realign our thinking. This psychological poison affects all of us, and even I once thought that using the word n*gga was ok to do. But there was also a point when I realized that it was "n*gga-like" thinking that led me to believe that I should refer to myself and my brother in the most degrading way imaginable. I then had to accept that my bad habit was not good for the soul of my community.

Russell, it's time for us to stop thinking like n*ggas. There are more intelligent and thoughtful ways for black men to reference themselves. You know it, I know it and so does everyone else. Let's get away from selling poison.

Dr. Boyce: Kris Kross, Weezy and Drugs: The Power of Really Good Marketing

In my 20 years of teaching in various business schools, there's one thing I know for sure: Marketing DOES work. The best kind of marketing is the stuff that doesn't look like marketing at all, like a viral Mountain Dew commercial, or a song on the radio where the word "Molly" is repeated over and over again, in a way that bangs down the door of your subconscious mind and plants itself into the deepest parts of your brain.

Oh, you don't know what Molly is? Just ask your teenage son or daughter. If they didn't know what it was last month, they now surely know what it is, where to get it, some friends who use it and might even know when they plan to try it themselves. This brand has been thoroughly introduced to nearly every teenager in America, especially the ones who love Trinidad James. In the words of former President George W. Bush, "Mission Accomplished."

You see, there's a reason that Reebok once paid Rick Ross millions of dollars to put his chubby little toes into their sneakers. It wasn't because he was training for the Olympics. They paid him money because he is what some might call an "urban influencer." Kids in the hood see

Reeboks on Rick's feet, and they go out and buy Reeboks themselves (even if they don't have any money). So, to those who don't think that repetitive messages in hip-hop have an impact on the subconscious thinking of our kids, I ask this: If kids imitate rappers based on what they wear on their feet, don't you think they might also pay even closer attention to the content of their music?

My point here is simple: None of us should be surprised that police are now saying that Chris Kelly, a member of the group Kris Kross, probably died from a drug overdose. Katt Williams blames his "little episodes" on bi-polar disorder without considering the possibility that extensive modification of your brain chemistry via drug use is likely going to exacerbate any pre-existing mental health condition.

We also shouldn't have been surprised when Lil Wayne went to the hospital (again) for "seizures." Rick Ross also went to the hospital a few months ago for seizures, and both men want you to believe that their conditions have nothing to do with their long histories of drug and alcohol abuse. I can't say for sure if all that "purple drank" Wayne's consuming is causing his seizures, but I can guarantee that it doesn't help. Oh, don't know what "purple drank" is? Just ask your teenage son, it's been extensively marketed to him already.

The rapper Nate Dogg died younger than most. Just a few years ago, Nate released a really hot song that ended with the words, "Hey hey hey hey......smoke weed everyday." I'm not sure if someone paid him to issue what sounded like a Public Service announcement promoting excessive marijuana consumption, but it surely had an impact.

Hip-hop on the radio (which isn't controlled by black people, it's only puppetry with black face) is now pushing a "go-hard" lifestyle, where staying high and drunk is a source of pride. The powers-that-be know that a young black man constantly seeking out his next high is probably not going to become the next Malcolm X; in fact, there is evidence that the CIA allowed drugs into the black community in response to the energy created during the civil rights movement. The only thing more effective than getting black men hooked on drugs is to be able to lock them up for drug possession. It must be a relief that we contribute so readily to our own oppression.

The point here is that when we see the fallout from the consistent promotion of drug use and alcohol consumption, we just might want to be a wee bit alarmed. Our kids might need to hear graphic stories about how many men and women are serving 30 year prison sentences for committing felonies that occurred while they were under the influence of one of the substances being promoted by artists nation-wide.

One young man, 19-year old Justin Jones, admitted that he deserved the death penalty after murdering someone when he "hit some weed" that was laced with PCP. When I see Justin, I see a man who could have (or might already be) someone's father. He could have been a great husband, attorney, or perhaps a black leader. His English was definitely broken, but there was a degree of intelligence, conscientiousness and naiveté that told me that had he been raised with the right messages, he could have been something other than another payday for the prison industrial complex.

I point people to an article on *RapRehab.com* which shows that many of the companies that own and market hip-hop labels and artists also have significant ownership stakes in private prisons. I'm not exactly sure what's going on, but the Finance professor in me says this ownership structure is probably no coincidence. So, the truth is that those who love black people and those who love the power of hip-hop may want to take up arms against companies that have spent billions of dollars seeking to control the minds of young black kids.

I'm sorry for the death of Chris Kelly and I'm honestly getting dressed for the funeral of Lil Wayne already (it should be happening any day now, I regrettably must admit). What bothers me most is that these are just two of the millions of brilliant black boys who had their brains destroyed before the third grade. Nothing great has ever been accomplished by people sitting around getting high and drunk every day, and these messages have ruined an entire generation.

Four Reasons Why I Really Want to See "A Different World" Come Back

There are various media reports that Debbie Allen is seeking to bring "A Different World" back to television. We're not sure what the status of her revival happens to be, but I am pretty damn excited about it. So, in order to celebrate the possibility of having one of the greatest shows on television brought back to the airwaves, I thought I'd make a quick list of reasons that I hope "A Different World" is brought back to life.

1) **The message was positive:** In a world where rappers use the words "b*tches and hoes" as if they were "peanut butter and jelly," it would be nice to see a show that talks about black women as empowered, educated and competent creatures, not just objects of degradation. Also, to contrast media that tells every black man that he should run as far away from a book as he possibly can, it would be nice to teach young black men that the brother with straight As is the coolest and most successful dude in the room.

2) **HBCUs need a boost:** The recent financial troubles of Morris Brown have the school on the brink of collapse, with several other HBCUs soon to follow. When the original

show came out over 20 years ago, HBCU attendance saw a huge bump due to the weekly dose of black college life being marketed on major network television. The psychological impact that "A Different World" had on young kids serves as additional evidence to refute the claims of those who sincerely believe that violent music has no effect on the psyches of our kids. Here's the newsflash: Media impacts the minds of those who absorb it at both the conscious and sub-conscious levels.

3) **The show can make money:** I sincerely doubt that NBC executives ever cared very much about HBCUs. The truth is that they care about MONEY. The fact that the network kept the show on for as long as they did is a reminder that it was a money-maker. Also, there are black films released regularly that are hugely profitable, including those made by Tyler Perry, Steve Harvey and even TD Jakes. So, if this model works in movies, it can also work on television. Additionally, there are more networks to choose from, making it easier to get the show back onto the airwaves.

4) **Because the show was amazing:** I don't know about you, but there are nights when I wonder what happened to the characters on "A Different World." Of course it's not

normal to think about fictional characters as if they are real people, but don't pretend like you don't miss them. Of course, the new show would likely feature a new generation of characters, but we have to confess that "A Different World" represents the golden age of black network television. The show was funny, cool, smart and positive. But then again, that's what black people are all about.

Ask Black America: Should Rihanna Be Concerned about Setting a Bad Example for Girls?

When it comes to the wild love affair between Rihanna and Chris Brown, there are a wide variety of opinions on whether or not the two should be together. Some say that she's an adult, and we should leave her alone. Others are saying that she sets a bad example for young women everywhere by conveniently overlooking the fact that Chris nearly killed her three years ago. Chris is not being judged in the same manner as Rihanna, largely because we've all pretty much decided that he is the abuser and not likely the one who is going to inject much common sense into this relationship. Some still have hope for Rihanna, but that hope is fleeting.

About 20 years ago, there was another couple that made headlines every week with a man by the last name of Brown. Bobby Brown and Whitney Houston were a lot like Chris and Rihanna: Two young R&B s*x symbols with money to burn and loads of fame. But the years slowly caught up with them: Whitney died long before her time, and Bobby has suffered from years of addiction and is a shadow of what he used to be. They too were defiant in their addiction to one another, even when that addiction cost them their careers or their lives.

So, beyond the long-term personal implications of being in an abusive relationship where you casually joke about getting high together, there is the public impact being made by your decisions. As the father of impressionable young women, I can testify that the things that Rihanna does certainly impacts young women, whether she cares or not. Also, there may be a lesson to learn about making poor relationship choices at an early age, for it'll be difficult to feel sorry for Rihanna and Chris when their chickens come home to roost.

Jay-Z Responds to Harry Belafonte: "My Presence is Charity" – Let Me Explain Why He's Wrong

Jay-Z is one of the most respected hip-hop artists in the world. His lyrical brilliance is second-to-none, and he does things on the mic that most of us could never dream of. Let's just get that out of the way right now.

But one interesting thing about money, power and fame is that it can make you very defensive and sometimes even a little arrogant. This week, Jay-Z spoke to *Rap Radar* about the recent challenge by activist and entertainer Harry Belafonte, where Harry said that Jay-Z and his lovely wife Beyonce could do more for black people than get us to shake our b*utts and buy their records.

Harry's words didn't fall on deaf ears, and Jay came back with a diss record during which he called Harry a "boy" and basically told him that his time of relevance is over. I personally felt that Jay's words were both inappropriate and disrespectful, and it seemed that quite a few others felt the same way.

In response to the Belafonte critique and subsequent backlash, here's what Jay-Z had to say:

> "I'm offended by that because first of all, this is going to sound arrogant, but my presence is charity. Just who I am, just like Obama is. Obama provides hope. Whether he does anything, that hope that he provides for a nation and outside of America is enough. Just being who he is. You're the first black president. If he speaks on any issue or anything, he should be left alone. Of course we want to challenge [Obama] to do better, but I felt like Belafonte just went about it wrong. The way he did it, within the media, and then he bigged up Bruce Springsteen. It was like, 'Whoa, you just sent the wrong message all around. You just bigged up the white guy against me in the white media.' I'm not saying that in a racial way. I'm saying what it was just the wrong way to go about it. My presence is charity! Just this guy who came from Marcy projects apartment 530C, to these places of me playing in Yankee stadium tonight."

Call me crazy, but I hear some of where Jay-Z is coming from. Belafonte's decision to attack Jay-Z likely triggered an automatic defense mechanism that most mega-celebs have to "brush their shoulders off" when haters come after them. A better approach might have been that of Oprah

Winfrey, who accepted Jay-Z for his imperfections, yet challenged him to do better. Oprah is joining a group of other billionaires who've all agreed to give half of their wealth to charity when they die. That's one of the things that makes her special in both physical and spiritual ways.

On the flip side of that, I stick to my original position that Jay-z should respect the fact that Harry is twice his age. Harry did more for black America before the age of 30 than Jay-Z will probably do for the rest of his life. He came along during a time when dignity mattered more than diamonds, and standing up for your people meant more than getting cozy with corporate America. In fact, he risked both his life and his freedom for the black community, and there isn't a celeb I can think of who would be willing to do the same thing today. Jay-Z grew up in an era where greed became God, so much of what we're discussing might be outside his sphere of understanding: I fully expect that he is going to ignore me.

I've never met Jay-Z, but I built a bridge to work closely with his friend, Russell Simmons. Our common ground leaned on the idea that we both believe that the black community cannot prosper without committing ourselves to ending the criminalization of young black men. I wish

Jay-Z had joined the 175 other celebrities who signed our open letter the president, but for some reason, he did not.

One thing I would hope is that Jay-Z is willing to allow himself to be educated on two points behind his statement about Belafonte. Without judging too harshly, here are two things that Hova needs to understand:

The first point is that your presence might be meaningful, but symbolism only means so much. Jay's comparisons to president Obama are very telling in that both of them seem to believe that it makes sense to compensate the black community with your face, so that they can "watch the throne" and dream about becoming big shots one day themselves. Sure, this might mean something to some people, but it can also be a cop out for a lack of courage and commitment to doing what is right.

An example would be a father who believes that he is being a good role model to his son by simply coming home every day and paying the bills, or a husband who thinks he gave a woman a gift by getting married and doing nothing else. But this doesn't include the value of spending time, making sacrifices, and all the other things that come along with being a good partner or parent. When it comes to public figures who've been given power and a voice, simply showing your face means nothing if your presence leads to little or no action on your part.

The second thing that Jay-Z might need to understand is that there is a difference between charity and activism. Charity is valuable, no question about that. But the black community isn't looking for Jay to fund a couple of scholarships or do a few free concerts. Black America needs public figures with testicular fortitude and the desire to stand up for them when they are suffering. Anyone who peeks at the quality of life data knows that, without question, black people are suffering in ways that are unimaginable. Jay-Z and Beyonce have become like the megapastors who roll to church in a Bentley while half of their congregation is starving to d***h.

Slavery wasn't ended with charity. The Civil Rights Movement didn't happen because Dr. King provided symbolism. Harry Belafonte never once believed that the depth of his obligation to his people simply meant showing his face and saying "Watch the throne b*tches and give me your last twenty dollars." Harry's actions meant connecting to the depth of his manhood, making tremendous sacrifices, marching, organizing, testifying, refusing to perform, boycotting, speaking out, taking risks and doing all that he could to prove himself to be a worthy soldier on the battlefield of equality.

Mind you, not every entertainer is expected to be a soldier like Harry Belafonte. He was certainly one of a kind. But Jay-Z can learn a thing or two from the Sports Illustrated poll which asked if Michael Jordan or Muhammad Ali was the greatest athlete of the 20th century: Both men are champions. Both men were the best in their sports. Both men are admired around the world. But when it was all said and done, the contest wasn't even close.

The reason that Ali dwarfed Michael Jordan is because for Michael, his inability to give to a cause greater than himself makes him a one-trick pony. All he is and ever will be is a great basketball player who sold a few gym shoes. Muhammad Ali transcended his sport and influenced people who've never seen a boxing match. He put his career on the line to save thousands of lives from the Vietnam War. He spoke up about racism during a time when his people were being beaten and killed just for being black. He sacrificed the peak of his career in order to stand up for his people. Unlike men like Jay-Z and Jordan, Ali never let a white man turn him into a boy by scaring him into silence. That's why he will always be "the greatest."

Jay-Z: Your people are suffering unemployment rates that are the worst we've seen in decades. We're being locked away in a mass incarceration epidemic that is as bad as the Jewish holocaust. Kids are finishing high school without even knowing how to read. Young black males who look like you are having their heads blown off on the way to school.

My question is: What in the h*ell are you gonna do about it? Just show your face and do a few cute little charity events? Or are you going to think like a man and stand up for the people you love? Your voice has tremendous power. You've got hundreds of millions of dollars in the bank. What in the world are you afraid of? That white people are going to take it all away from you? It's one thing for a poor man to be fearful of taking political risks for important causes, but when you are nearly a billionaire and just as fearfully silent, that is tantamount to a form of mental illness.

The final point I'd make to Jay-Z is this: You came out of the Marcy Projects in Brooklyn, defeated the odds, and rose to the top of the world. This feat didn't go unnoticed by the millions of 12-year old Jay-Z wannabes, many of whom live in the same projects that you came from. But the data says that 99.9999% of those young men are never going to get a record deal, marry a woman as gorgeous as Beyonce or fly private jets to foreign lands. A larger percentage of them are going to end up d**d, in prison, uneducated, unemployed, addicted to drugs and a*****l, and all the other things that happen to countless young black men across the country.

If your massive wealth, power, influence and fame only helps one or two people who came out of Marcy projects and ignores the other thousands of black children who live in the same situation, then the blessings you've received from God have been wasted. God put you on this earth to be a king, but you've allowed those around you to convince you to be a mascot.

When you're standing on the shoulders of giants, you can't choose to be a spiritual dwarf. We've got 99,000 problems, and you're only focused on one. That's why Harry Belafonte dissed you.

After Belafonte Criticism, Beyonce, Jay-Z Step Up for Trayvon Martin

The people have spoken, and the Carters have answered. Shortly after the stinging public criticism of her husband's diss verse against Harry Belafonte, there's been an uptick in the activism category on the busy schedules of Beyonce and Jay-Z. This week, as the world expressed its rage about the 'not guilty' verdict in the trial of George Zimmerman, Beyonce and Jay showed up to lend their support at a Trayvon Martin rally in New York.

Then, going beyond the call of duty, Beyonce posted a petition in support of Trayvon on her website. These were some of the words on the petition:

> "We are still struggling with the issue of inequality and the lack of value for a black man's life. Trayvon Martin's most basic civil right, the right to live, was violated. We have made so much progress and cannot allow hatred and racism to divide us. When we all join together, people of all races, we have the power to change the world we live in. We must fight for Trayvon the same way the generation before us fought for Emmett Till. I joined over 570,000 people

> in signing the petition below, and hopefully you will, too."

Making matters even more interesting, Beyonce posted a picture of her visiting Ebenezer Baptist Church in Atlanta and remembering the important contributions of the great Dr. Martin Luther King, Jr. I certainly hope the reflection was sincere, and that Beyonce is growing in her understanding of the black struggle, as well as her role and opportunity to be a part of it. She should also learn from her friend Oprah Winfrey that sometimes, fighting for what you believe in means being strategically tough and controversial.

There is no proof that Belafonte's words had anything to do with the Carter's actions, but it's awfully curious that this is the first time that I can recall Beyonce supporting any petition of any kind that might somehow be interpreted as an attack on the Obama Administration. Obama Administration Senior Adviser Valerie Jarrett takes her celebrity friendships seriously, and tends to interpret even modest requests from President Obama to be tantamount to black treason. So, one shouldn't take lightly Beyonce's decision to put her name behind a petition that asks the Obama Administration to do anything. They don't seem to appreciate any degree of African American discontent.

I'm always smiling when celebrities step their game up, and I am happy with what the Carters have done this week. Now, I only hope that Beyonce can convince her husband to never again write lyrics insulting one of the greatest civil rights icons in history. Harry Belafonte's sacrifices as an entertainer nearly left him unemployed, broke and d**d. He is older than Jay-Z and Beyonce put together, so they should respect his wisdom and see his tough love as a call to arms for a community that is in deep peril. For all of the money that black folks spend traveling to Beyonce and Jay-Z concerts, I hope they will remember that support should be a two-way street, and not just one where your audience is asked to "Watch the Throne" while you're sitting in it, draped in diamonds and gold.

On a similar note, the Trayvon Martin tragedy wasn't just painful just because of what happened to Trayvon. It was symbolic of the millions of other Trayvon Martins around the country, many of whom are racially profiled, making them more likely to be stopped, arrested and incarcerated, even when they commit the same crimes as whites. Just a

night in jail can scar and destroy a person for life, and too many of our kids are being fed into the criminal justice system at an early age, either as a victim or as a perpetrator (the case of straight A student Gabbriella Calhoun is a perfect example of how good kids are destroyed by police who abuse their authority).
As a result of consistent racial profiling by police, millions of black men are part of the criminal justice system, and even more have died. These are the men who were meant to be husbands and fathers in our communities, so we cannot allow their fates to be determined by an imbalanced and unjust system. The same thing is true for all of the women who are now being affected. This is destroying our families, and ultimately our community. You only need to hear the messages in our music as a reflection of what has happened to black America as a result of being polluted by a corrupt criminal justice system.

These were the images that were discussed when I spoke extensively with Russell Simmons about our joint campaign to stop mass incarceration. Over 175 celebrities, scholars, and activists signed the letter that Russell and I wrote to President Obama, and our sense of urgency was driven by the fact that the black community is in a state of crisis.

Any statistician will tell you that when it comes to unemployment rates, urban violence, educational inequality and incarceration rates, black America has hit rock bottom. We've gotten used to the idea that our families are falling apart, that people can't find jobs, that our kids can't read and that every other black man is going to prison. We cannot accept our g******e to be part of business as usual, and Trayvon's d***h is the social alarm clock we need to understand just how deep this problem goes. But as with any alarm clock, you can't just hit the snooze button. You've got to get your black a** out of bed.

Times as dire as these require every soldier to line up and be prepared for battle: Beyonce and Jay-Z included—No justice, no peace, no excuses. It's a new day in Black America.

Tough Question: Can You Name One Positive Stereotype About Black People?

Stereotypes are usually not a good thing, but for some, they can make life easier. Jews are often stereotyped as being good with money and wealth-building. Asians are stereotyped for being math geniuses. Even Latin Americans can be stereotyped as being hard-working.

If someone were to ask you to *name one positive stereotype about black people*, would you be able to do so?

If you're like most people, you probably can't. We do get some stereotypes thrust upon us, like being able to run fast and jump high (someone even said that we are well-endowed, as if that's some kind of meaningful talent that you can put on a resume), but those are not stereotypes that typically lead to wealth building, at least not for most of us. If anything, athletic ability can sometimes cause men and women to waste their brain power and educational opportunities chasing hoop dreams or some obscure chance of getting into the NFL.

The Janks Morton film, "Hoodwinked" explores some of these issues. I encourage you to take a look at the trailer.

I was very impressed with the film and appreciate that Roland Martin and Tom Joyner supported the effort by featuring the film on their shows. The premieres have sold out thus far, and we're excited to be able to make this intellectual contribution to the African American community. I am in the film, along with four other outstanding scholars who care about the self-images of black men: Marc Lamont Hill, Steve Perry, Ivory Toldson and Jawanza Kunjufu.

The film is starting to take off, and I'm excited. Once black men begin learning how great we can be, then this will surely bust the lid of opportunity wide open. The scariest black man in America is not the thug on the corner. Actually, it's the highly-educated, conscientious black man who knows no fear.

Chapter 2

The Athlete: Symbol of Power, Privilege and Popular Culture

Notes from a Finance Professor: Why Black Athletes Go Broke

I recently noticed that my homeboy TJ Holmes at BET recently had a show about professional athletes who find their finances in the toilet. I consider this to be an interesting and relevant topic, just the kind of thing that BET needs to show. As a Finance Professor who's been hanging around college campuses for over 20 years, I've seen a few things that I think might serve as some of the root causes as to why so many black athletes go broke.

Yes, we know some of the white guys go broke too, but I'm not talking to them right now. Brother, I'm talking to you. Based on my experience as a Finance guy, a former athlete and a black man, I can name at least five reasons that so many athletes end up right where they started:

1) **A lack of education:** The saddest habit that some athletes have embraced is the idea that being good at sports means that you don't have to have a good education. Guess what? Most of the people who make the real money in the NBA and NFL are guys like my friend Billy Hunter, head of the NBA Players Association. I spoke with Billy for a very long time before our Fatherhood panel in Harlem two weeks ago, and Billy made it abundantly

clear that he made a lot more money with his law degree than he did by catching a football. The old saying "a fool and his money will soon part ways" is quite accurate, as your Harvard educated attorney/business manager will keep making millions long after your knees wear out.

2) **The arrogance and invincibility complex:** It's easy to think that the next paycheck will be bigger than the last, or that your NFL career is going to last 40 years. But the fact is that one day it's all going to slow down and perhaps come to an end. Just ask Terrell Owens and Chad Johnson—I mean Ochocinco—I mean Johnson—I mean Mr. Lozada. When all you are is an athlete, you have little value to your overseers once you can no longer play.

3) **A lack of discipline:** For all the brilliance and discipline I've seen displayed on the football field and basketball court, I don't always see the same discipline in every area of the athlete's life. What young brothers need to realize is that there are basically four vices that lead to the downfall of nearly every great man in history: s*x, drugs, alcohol and gambling. If you are gluttonous and excessive in any of these four areas, you risk losing everything because of a few poor mistakes. I don't have to mention many of the

athletic tragedies that have occurred in recent weeks for you to understand what I'm talking about.

4) **Sloppy family planning:** You think you're the man because you can get any woman you want huh? Well guess what brother? The ladies want you too! In fact, they're going to keep wanting a piece of you long after baby mama number four is raising your child and trying to get you sent to jail for not being able to pay child support. I am an 18 year veteran of the Draconian child support system and I can say from first-hand experience, you don't want to go there.

5) **Making it rain, popping bottles and whatever else 2Chainz told you to do in his last album:** I swear that if I write one more article about an athlete dying, getting arrested or doing something stupid at the club, outside the club or on the way home from the club, I'm going throw up on my computer screen. There is no rule saying that every black man has to behave like a jackass on the weekends and drink until he loses control of his faculties. Most stupid crimes that get people sent away for years are committed while under the influence. Don't throw it all away by following the crowd.

These are my perspectives, take em or leave em, but I know there is tremendous hope for black men. For every Trinidad James or Jevon Belcher, there's a Lupe Fiasco or Etan Thomas. Smart brothers lead the way and people who choose to embrace the ignorance are the ones who end up telling their sons, "Don't do what I did." Teach yourself, your kids and those you mentor that life is all about making good choices, having good values and being a good person. There's really no other way around it.

Deaths of NFL Players This Week Speak Volumes about Self-Destructive Culture

Dallas Cowboys defensive lineman Josh Brent has been charged with intoxication manslaughter after he was involved in an accident this weekend that killed his teammate, Jerry Brown. This is the second tragedy that has hit the NFL in recent days. Most of us know about the death of Jovan Belcher of the Kansas City Chiefs, who killed his girlfriend and himself, also on a weekend rampage.

During our panel on black male fatherhood in New York City this week, I spoke with several NBA players, an NFL player and NBA Player's Association Executive Director Billy Hunter about the culture of black male athletes. One of the things that has consistently concerned me is the culture of self-destructive behavior which seems to walk hand-in-hand with being a black male athlete. Popping bottles at the club, "getting it in" with random women and putting yourself into one horrible situation after another has become almost a requirement for young men trying to fit into this culture.

Let me be one of the first to publicly say, "This sh*t is stupid." There's no point in being polite about this conversation, since people are dying because we refuse to speak up.

The common factors in both the Belcher murder-suicide and the death of Jerry Brown are that a) they both occurred on the weekend, b) they both involved excessive amounts of alcohol and c) they were probably leaving "da club" or some other social gathering when their lives came to an end. As a result, one black man is in prison, two black men are dead, one black woman is also dead and at least two black babies are going to grow up without their fathers.

We owe it to our young men to speak candidly about the dangers of excessive alcohol consumption and teach them the value of critical thinking when it comes to avoiding the many creative ways to destroy your life and the lives of those you care about. Right before his death, Jerry Brown was openly questioning the value of "the fast life" on his Facebook page, wondering if this life is conducive to his being a good father and husband one day.

I would have loved to sit down with this brother to say, "No man, it's not. Your daughter, girlfriend, and mother all need you to be the best man you can be. I don't care what you're hearing on the radio every morning, but nothing good has ever been accomplished by an entire segment of the population that spends all of its time getting high and drunk every other day. Brother, you are better than that."

One of the reasons I respect former New York Giant David Tyree is that he speaks openly about how alcoholism put him in a jail cell just a few years ago. During our panel in Harlem, Tyree shared his experience as a cautionary tale for young men who don't understand the value of thinking outside the slave box. We may no longer be physically enslaved, but many of us are psychologically enslaved by the media which presents imagery of black men as animal-like creatures with no productive direction. Another panelist, former Washington Wizards player Etan Thomas, said it best when he said that, "They do these things because they are afraid of us and what might happen if we were to realize our truest potential."

Now, because no one, to my knowledge, had a candid, honest conversation with Jerry Brown about the dangers of "the fast life," he died before having the chance to figure out that this life just isn't worth it. There are more productive and fulfilling things to do on a Friday night than to sit around popping bottles at the club. We must share this message with our young men EVERY CHANCE WE GET.

Additionally, we must rethink the culture surrounding many young black men who define themselves as nothing but dumb jocks. We must empower them to use their platforms, wealth and opportunity to do great things and not to transform themselves into victims of an oppressive partnership. Black male athletes are among the strongest, fastest, most intelligent and most courageous warriors in the entire black community. They must not be allowed to be transformed into sad little sheep.

Black Athletes Should Never Take Pride in Being Ignorant

I received a phone call from a friend who teaches elementary school. She told me that she'd spent the week excited about the fact that some college basketball players were coming to her school to eat lunch with the kids. She thought that her inner city students would gain from the chance to be mentored by the men they saw on TV.

Was she ever wrong. The men who came to her school left a less-than-favorable impression: Their chopped up speaking skills made her wonder if they'd gotten past a fifth grade reading level; some of them didn't even know if they were juniors or seniors in college, and most of them barely knew their major (which was usually General Studies or one of those other "interesting" majors that happen to be chosen by half the basketball team).

As my friend described her situation, I thought about how far too often, collegiate athletics becomes nothing more than a virtual wasteland for African American men. Stuck on hoop dreams that will never materialize, many of these men throw away any chance or desire to obtain a meaningful education, and simultaneously buy into a culture of self-indulgent, counter-productive behavior that ends up making some of them almost worthless to our community.

You know the behavior I'm talking about, which is driven by commercialized hip-hop (that's why rappers and athletes love to roll together): "I got many hoes," "pass the weed n*gga," "Shawty, I ain't been to class in like two weeks" type of stuff. Rather than the strong black man who leads his family and community, these men are encouraged to become the weed-smoking, pistol-poppin, club-strollin, woman-gettin playa who grows old sitting in his girlfriend's living room in his drawz playing Xbox all day. How deep they fall into the stereotype just depends on how much of the cultural kool-aid they choose to drink.

What's so interesting about this behavior is that it is in stark contrast to the way these men line up like soldiers on their chosen academic plantations, running offensive schemes to precision, practicing their hearts out and displaying Einstein-like brilliance as they master complicated playbooks that are 200 pages thick. They are managed like well-trained circus animals, working to the bone to fill the coffers of an athletic overseer who stands to earn millions from the team's next bowl-game or Final Four appearance.

Of course I'm not talking about every college athlete. Some athletes understand the game of life, and are protected from the desire to sell their soul for someone else's economic dream. They understand the value in being both athletic and intelligent, and look forward to their futures as strong husbands and fathers.

But most of us know the brothers who "just don't get it." These are the men who, like pigs being led to slaughter, have bought into a lifestyle that is going to lead to their demise and the destruction of everything they love. Some of them end up in prison, some end up getting shot at a club during a "fight wit dat n*gga who was talking sh*t," and even more end up as unemployed, uneducated, washed-up ex-NBA wannabes seeking out dead fantasies in the bottom of a bottle.

Is the NCAA partially to blame for this? Absolutely. They seem a lot more concerned when a player affects their revenue stream than they are about that player being educated or fairly compensated. But are our men to blame as well? Most definitely – in life, some of us are victims and some of us are volunteers. The players are just as happy as their coaches to sign the lopsided contracts that give away nearly all of their labor and educational rights in exchange for a little "shine," "swag," and "ballerability." Even in prostitution, there are some situations where both the pimp and the hoe are happy with the arrangement. Collegiate athletics is the perfect pimp-hoe prototype and it makes me incredibly sad. Perhaps one day we will wake up and smell the exploitation.

The NCAA Continues to Pimp Students and the Rest of Us

NCAA athletics has become the new prohibition—the illogical construct that creates a destructive underground economy because leadership is being guided by an illusion of what should be, rather than confronting the NCAA for what it really is: a professional sports league. Some of our most highly educated figures within academia are forced to convince themselves that a multi-billion dollar sports entertainment behemoth should be able to get away with not paying its primary employees.

The smart white men running the NCAA also took enough history classes to easily see the parallels with slavery: An oppressive and unethical institution that everyone knows to be a farce, yet it continues to survive because it would be entirely too costly to shut it down. It's hard to walk away from a billion dollars per year, even if you have to be a criminal and pathological liar in order to protect it. Actually, the NCAA earns more ad revenue in March Madness than the NFL, NBA and Major League Baseball earn during their post-seasons; that much money would tempt any of us to become crooks.

NCAA athletes are not slaves, we know this, but exploitation is a continuum, not a dichotomy. Even the five-year old child working in a Chinese sweat shop has the right to stay home from work if he chooses to do so. But staying home would be to his family's detriment. If one allows the beast of capitalism to operate in an unregulated manner, we quickly find that allegedly free human beings are ultimately left with no option but to work for an unfair wage. While the NCAA spends millions monitoring the choices of college athletes, almost no one monitors the actions of the NCAA to ensure that their labor practices are consistent with American values. As a result, they are as un-American as Kim Jong II and Mahmoud Ahmadinejad.

NCAA President Mark Emmert, who earns nearly a million dollars per year off the families of NCAA athletes, has maintained the lie of the league by stating publicly that college athletes will not be paid under his regime. He's the latest overseer in a system that loves the idea that in a racist society like this one, Black men should be happy with whatever scraps you choose to give them. He and others are allowed to get away with their exploitation because most Americans are as unoffended by the exploitation of Black families as they are by the slaughtering of chickens at KFC.

"I don't see why they should get anything more than what I get," says the typical white kid on any campus USA. "They already get special treatment and I'm sick of it. I'd love to be able to go to school for free."

Well, I would tell that kid this: As soon as you grow to be seven feet tall and can score 20 points per game on a nationally televised show that draws 10 million viewers and $30 million dollars in revenue, then I'll speak up for your mother too. I've always been amazed at how the nerdy Chemistry major somehow believes that he's made as strong of a financial contribution to the university as the basketball star who draws tens of millions of dollars in advertising. If that's the case, then I should be paid the same as Will Smith.

It's interesting that the same NCAA administrators who stand adamantly against the idea of compensating a family for their child's labor have no problem collecting their own massive salaries every year. If coaches, administrators and commentators are not interested in taking a vow of poverty, then athletes' families should not have to do so either. The notion that an administrator or coach deserves to be fairly compensated while the individual doing the work does not is nothing more than the same second class citizenship that African Americans have faced for the last 400 years—simply asking for equality is out of the question.

So, not only does the NCAA continue to pimp the athletes, it also pimps the rest of us. Their multi-million dollar ad campaigns (again, financed by the labor of the athletes) have convinced us that it's scandalous when a player (worth over $10 million dollars to his university) signs autographs in exchange for a free tattoo (as with the suspended players from Ohio State last year). They paint "street agents" who share money with an athlete's struggling family as criminals, while simultaneously making it clear that they could care less if the player's mother and siblings starve to death. They've convinced us that they are the good guys—the benevolent overseers who are giving these pathetic Negroes something that is a far cry better than anything these kids could get from "the hood."

While NCAA officials might hope our response would be, "Thank you massa, that's mighty kind of you," a better reaction might be, "Why am I doing all the work and you're keeping all the money?" But then again, there's a reason slave owners didn't want slaves to learn how to read—it's for the same reason NCAA administrators want

Black men focused on bling, women and fame rather than intricate business models and labor rights. When an oppressed group of people start asking hard questions, it makes for a very uncomfortable conversation.

The bottom line is that NCAA athletes deserve the same labor rights as the rest of us. They should also be able to unionize and engage in collective bargaining. There is no logical reason why athletes shouldn't receive liberties that are freely given to those who aren't doing the work to earn the money.

Slavery didn't end because slave owners decided to do the right thing. It ended because those who'd become possessed by the demons of capitalism had their power forcibly taken away from them. Athletes, parents and concerned citizens must file lawsuits, organize, protest, and refuse to play until they are fairly compensated. Money and power are typically not given away without a fight, and if you're not willing to fight for your freedom, then you do not truly deserve it.

What Makes LeBron James One of the Great Ones

For the most part, the NBA bores me, but that hasn't always been the case. I was a typical black kid who grew up on the basketball court, learning the ins and outs of the game. So, even though I only watch the last five minutes of the last game of every championship series, I am still able to keep up with what's going on.

Also, I've become more intrigued with the behind-the-scenes workings of the NBA, where black athletes all too often have their freedom and their fortunes stripped by guys in fancy suits who went to Harvard. I witnessed this foolishness up close when I supported former NBA Union head Billy Hunter when he was pushed out of the league. What I learned is that when you give hundreds of millions of dollars to guys who are only focused on dribbling a basketball, there are going to be others jockeying for position to control them as if they are farm animals. Some NBA players understand what's going on, but quite a few of these brothers don't know and don't care until it's too late.

I first saw LeBron James play about 9 or 10 years ago. He was taking on Oak Hill Academy, a basketball farm that disguises itself as an educational institution. LeBron was bigger, taller and more skilled than his teammates and seemed to single-handedly elevate his team to defeat a school that actively recruits the best players in the country. Shortly after the win against Oak Hill, I watched LeBron control the McDonald's All-Star game like a father playing basketball with his five-year old kids: He didn't try to score very many points, but seemed to decide who should get to score next. I was astonished, since he clearly managed the entire game on both ends of the floor.

My initial impression of LeBron was that he was going to be something very special in the NBA. He wasn't a regular All American, but the kind of athlete who could do something truly special. Ironically, it wasn't just his talent that got my attention. I was equally impressed with his poise during interviews, his willingness to be a good teammate, and the way he made himself better by helping others to get better too. He was no Michael Jordan because Jordan was incredibly selfish early in his career. Instead, LeBron came off to me as an only child of a single parent who yearned for the camaraderie that comes from being part of a unit that is greater than himself.

As I've watched LeBron go through the ups and downs to win his first two championships, I have to give him credit for his personal and professional growth. Most of us have no idea what it's like to already be one of the best athletes on the planet, but to still have almost no margin of error when it comes to refining nearly every single aspect of your game. For LeBron, a couple of missed jump shots or free throws alters his entire legacy. It doesn't matter if he is 98% as good as he could have been, since that last 2% can kill you.

Despite these hurdles, LeBron persisted, plodding away to work on his weaknesses despite all of his extraordinary strengths. He learned that there is a difference between being the best and being at your best. He made the sacrifice of taking a major pay cut to join the Miami Heat alongside other players who could help him win championships. He took over when his team needed him, but continued to make others around him into better players. He did what it took to be the absolute best he could be.

My point here is not to engage in any kind of hero worship over the man who just won a title. It is to say that there are things many of us can learn from LeBron's big win.

Victories on this level aren't just physical ones, but require an Einstein-like degree of intelligence, a borderline psychotic level of devotion toward achieving your goal, nerves of steel when everything is one the line and laser-like focus to see through the distractions to remain obsessed on the prize. When I saw LeBron James on the basketball court, I didn't just see an athlete; actually, I saw a full-grown man taking what he wanted in spite of the fact that there were scores of world class athletes trying to get the same thing.

Most of us can learn from LeBron's spirit, persistence, determination and unwillingness to rest on his laurels. He also teaches us that, even when you're already the best in the game, you might still have to push harder than you'd ever imagined to get to the mountain top. The brother deserves to be commended for his accomplishments and I congratulate him on his success. Way to go LeBron, I'm proud of you.

Former NFL Star Warren Sapp Begging for Relief from His Five Baby Mamas

Ex-NFL superstar Warren Sapp has fallen upon hard times lately. The former Miami Hurricane great is finding that child support is not as much fun as making babies, and is now begging the courts to give him a reduction in the 2,500 per month he's paying one of the many women with whom he has fathered a child.

According to TMZ, Sapp filed paperwork requesting that his support obligations to Angela Sanders be dropped from the existing obligation of $2,500 per month, which should be chump change for a player who once signed a 7-year, $36.6 million dollar contract with the Oakland Raiders. For the record, that means that he earned over $14,000 a day, or about $429,000 per month, making $2,500 seem pale in comparison.

Obviously, Sanders is a little bit irritated by Sapp's request, since she made an agreement back in 2000 that the support would not be modified based on changes in income. At the time, she could have easily demanded as much as $10,000 per month, but instead took a modest amount that probably made her look stupid to her friends. So, the woman doesn't appear to be anyone's gold digger, and some would say that a millionaire should be paying far more to take care of his children.

Years later, after filing for bankruptcy protection and blowing all of his money on all kinds of stupid stuff, including 240 pairs of rare Air Jordans, Sapp is now whining to the courts for sympathy, even though they may end up putting his b**t in jail. Not only does Sapp owe big money to Sanders, but he's got four other mothers standing line, hands on their hips, wondering why the checks stopped coming in.

As a Finance Professor, I often cringe when I see how young brothers allow their arrogance to lead them to make horrible life decisions that leave them destitute, depressed, marginalized and possibly incarcerated. You're the big man on campus when you're catching passes on TV and hip hop music teaches you that "a real n*gga gotta keep his hoes in check." So, you're running through women like Black Friday sales at Walmart, always forgetting that chickens (and baby mamas) always come home to roost.

Years later, when the financial party is over and none of the teams are blowing up your phone the way they used to, you find yourself with little education, no good investments, and a long list of creditors, dependents and "ignant" financial obligations. That's when the hero has turned into a zero, and you get to spend the next 40 years paying the price for a series of unintelligent and exceedingly arrogant decisions (there were surely many people who tried to give Sapp good advice along the way, but dollar bills up to your ears can make you hard of hearing).

A full 78% of professional athletes end up going broke, much of this due to inadequate financial education and poor family planning. The NFL's financial responsibility seminars aren't doing the job, and these men who threw away all of their educational opportunities for the chance to risk permanent brain damage often find that a) there are easier ways to make money than this, and b) an uneducated man and his money will usually part ways.

I'm not here to beat up on Warren Sapp, for I wish him well. Instead, I'd rather encourage all of us to see the life of Warren Sapp as a living, breathing textbook on how to engage in good life management. Here are a couple of things we can learn from this latest episode of the Maury Povich Show for Negroes:

1) **No matter what you do, always get a good education:** Athletes, I hate to say it, are used up and distributed like cattle. The athlete is almost never as well off as his Harvard-educated attorney, and it's shameful that so many black men are taught that the false lottery ticket of sports is their only way to financial security. Remaining uneducated only opens the door for a smart person to steal all your money while you're at the club gulping bottles of Patron and creating baby mamas with 2Chainz playing in the background. All such forms of coonery should be outlawed and all violators should be slapped on sight.

2) **Be thoughtful about where you spread your seed:** The rule of thumb for the thoughtless, perpetually aroused young male is this: "If she looks good, and she offers, then I'm gonna hit that." But we often forget that irresponsibility in the bedroom can lead to enough STDs to turn you into a walking CDC alert, and also lead you to be strapped onto a person you barely know or care about for the next 18 years. Be smart about your choices when it comes to the opposite gender, for these choices play a tremendous role in shaping the trajectory of your life.

It's time to change the paradigm of the black athlete in America instead of repeating the same old story. By educating ourselves and each other, we can create progress instead of going backward. While the stories about men like Warren Sapp are blasted all over the media, we should also consider the stories of brilliant men like Allan Houston (former NY Knick) and Etan Thomas (Washington Wizards), who not only made sound financial decisions, but are also extraordinary role models, very well-educated and outstanding family men. I am moderating a panel on fatherhood at Abyssinian Baptist Church in Harlem with both men and I swell up with pride when I see black male athletes using their powerful platforms to do something other than to serve as a puppet for corporate America: The black community is suffering, with the black male at risk of extinction—we need our best, brightest and baddest to lend their voices to the people they love.

The life you live tomorrow is created by the choices you make today. Learning from the good and bad decisions of those who came before you is critical to your survival. But living the fast life without proper planning is like driving 100 miles per hour while wearing a blind fold: The crash is both painful and inevitable.

Vince Young, Chad Johnson, Terrell Owens: A Predictable Cycle of Self-Destruction

I remember seeing a picture of NFL player Vincent Young on the cover of *ESPN The Magazine* a few years ago. The image was taken shortly after Young won the NCAA championship for the Texas Longhorns, the institution that has made billions on the backs of unpaid black athletes. On the cover of the magazine were the words "I was born to play football at The University of Texas."

When I saw the quote on that cover, I knew that Young was doomed. Since that time, Vincent Young has been cut from the Buffalo Bills, possibly ending his NFL career. He became depressed and suicidal a few years ago after losing his starting spot with the Tennessee Titans. He has also gotten some attention for blowing $30 million dollars in six years by "making it rain" at the club and reportedly spending $5,000 per week at The Cheesecake Factory.

Young isn't the first, or the last, professional athlete to blow through money like he didn't want it. Chad Johnson, Terrell Owens and Allen Iverson are some other recent examples, as we get to watch our nation's gladiators melt down into little punks as they cry about the fact that they've lost it all.

The reason that I felt sorry for Vince when I saw that magazine cover is that I realized that this was a man who has shaped his entire identity around sports. He sees no other value that he can add to humanity that goes beyond throwing a football to entertain white people. There is a good chance that education has fallen on the backburner, and there is also a chance that he's engaged in the other destructive habits that can pollute the life of an athlete: sexual promiscuity, excessive consumption of drugs and alcohol, financial irresponsibility and other poor life choices.

Then, years after that athlete sits at the top of the world, he finds his life and his soul in the pits of hell. This is the story that can sometimes be told before it even happens, and I only hope that one day, we can learn from the mistakes of others.

The fact is that it's easier to become a surgeon than to become a professional football player. It's easier to become a high paid attorney than a rap star. A person has a much easier path to wealth by being a business owner than by trying to get into the NBA. Also, without education, you're lost. The wealthy athlete who can barely read is sure to be ripped off by his Harvard-educated business manager, who can replace him with another kid from the ghetto next year.

By not thinking about his life and choices off the field, Vince Young has created a life full of regrets. He, like so many other athletes, signed up for a life of slavery and an existence that makes him only a shadow of the man that he could have been. Any black man who walks away from education and the ability to engage in leadership and critical thinking makes himself as worthless as the crack head on the corner, in large part because he is choosing to destroy himself and neglect his community by not using his powerful platform for a productive purpose. There was a time when athletes prided themselves in being leaders of the community, but now, too many athletes are too busy Buck-dancing for a chance to get a Reebok commercial.

I love my brothers and I love sports, but we should all decide that we hate the embracing of ignorance. It's time to make a change.

50 Cent and Floyd Mayweather are the New Tyson and Tupac: Will Their Story End the Same Way?

You may have read about the decision of the rapper 50 Cent (aka Curtis Jackson) to jump into the fight promotions business. Observers are stating that it is a strong possibility that 50 Cent made this move so that he could work with one of his best friends, World Champion Floyd Mayweather. Mayweather is astonishingly quick and arguably the greatest boxer on the planet. With 50 Cent being a brilliant businessman and possibly the greatest self-promoter on earth, it's hard to imagine that the partnership can be anything but extraordinary.

Another thing I like about the Mayweather-Jackson alliance is that it allows the massive amounts of money being made in the fight game to stay within the black community. While a black man can screw you just as quickly as a white guy (see Don King), at least this situation allows for black families to be fed from the talent of black athletes. This contrasts with what I hate most about the NCAA, the most exploitative free labor scheme in America other than the prison industrial complex. Moves like the one by Mayweather and Jackson show that brothers are starting to understand that the real money makers in sports are not the guys on the field; actually, they are the guys in the back office who went to graduate school.

When I see the budding friendship between "Fiddy" and Money Mayweather, I am reminded of the consistent parallels between the worlds of hip hop and sports for black males in America. I think about the close friendship between Jay-Z and LeBron James, and other alliances that remind of us how these two worlds overlap and formulate this awkward, sometimes self-destructive, hyper-masculine pseudo-culture that is defined by shooting hoops, busting caps and busting rhymes. When there is a rapper at the club, he may very likely be tailed by an athlete or two, and between the two of them are the scores of nameless wannabes who just enjoy hanging around (e.g. NBA player Tony Parker getting cut in the eye at the brawl between Chris Brown and Drake).

When I see Money Mayweather hanging out with Fiddy, I am reminded of another intriguing friendship between the late Tupac Shakur and Mike Tyson. Pac and Iron Mike were very similar to Fiddy and Money Mayweather: They both had a mutual respect for the other man's heart, strength and charisma, and they also seemed to have a legitimate bond built on common struggles to overcome a great deal of adversity on their climbs to the top. Also like Mayweather and 50 Cent, they had trouble with the law. We know how the story of Tupac and Tyson ended. Both of them went to jail for long periods of time, and both of them tried to make a comeback. One of them died physically and the other died both spiritually and professionally. That which could have been legendary instead ended up extraordinarily tragic. The inability to make good decisions and overcome personal demons ruined both of these men and the moment that could have lasted forever was as fleeting as a one night stand.

When I see the brilliance and skill of 50 Cent partnered with the amazing talent of Mayweather, I see tremendous potential. I am especially impressed that they went a step further than Pac and Tyson and actually translated their friendship into a business relationship. But I am also disturbed that their lives can sometimes be filled with the kind of drama that can only be created by the cultural tornado of the African American male: Where it seems that you're more likely to end up dead, in prison, or in some other unfortunate situation because you're engaging in unhealthy responses to the dysfunction all around you.

Mayweather's stint in jail right now, which threatens to ruin his entire career, is a perfect case-in-point.

I hope that when Mayweather gets out of jail, he finds a way to stay out. I pray that these men can balance their natural bravado with the ability to make decisions that are going to sustain them spiritually and financially for the rest of their lives. I don't want Mayweather boxing until he's 45-years old and giving himself brain damage so he can pay the IRS, get out of bankruptcy and pay off five different baby's mamas. I don't want to hear that 50 Cent was shot on his way out of a night club after a fight with a gang member hanging out with a rival from another record label. Instead, I want to hear a story about how these young brothers at the top of their games went on to have amazing careers, growing old with as much style and class as they had when they were young.

The story of 50 Cent and Floyd Mayweather must end better than the one about Tupac and Tyson. We've got to take our game to the next level and continue to think in a more strategic and disciplined fashion. I wish these men the best of luck in their new venture and hope that Mayweather knocks a few people out in the process. But most importantly, it is the battles outside the ring that are going to be the most challenging, and they have to be sure to win those too.

Chapter 3

Economic Power, Black Youth and the Future of the Black Community

African Americans Must Occupy Wall Street

This week, I plan to head to New York City to join scores of American citizens who've decided that Wall Street should be confronted for the financial crimes that have been committed against the American people. It is an awkward reunion for me as a Finance Professor, since I have hundreds of former students who've gone on to make millions as Wall Street employees. So, perhaps it is because of my intimate understanding of the gospel of Finance that I can also see the dangers of creating a society that has come to believe that making money is the trump card that justifies nearly all sins against humanity, almost like the doctor who can tell when the patient has become addicted to the drug that was originally designed to heal him.

There are a long list of reasons that all of us should be concerned, disappointed and even angry about what Wall Street has done to our country. The real wage of the average American worker has remained stagnant, while the gap between the rich and the poor has risen to levels that are unsustainable in nearly any civilized society. We live under the illogical reality that those who caused the financial crisis by taking unnecessary risks were the first ones to be bailed out by politicians who are enslaved by campaign contributions and lobbying groups. Labor unions have been undermined throughout the nation, and while the joblessness problems persists, corporations are sitting on trillions in capital that could be used to hire American workers.

I am honored to be an American when I see that thousands of us have simply taken our country back from those who've denied their responsibility to properly regulate the power of capitalism in our society. Free enterprise can be a wonderful thing, but when capitalism is not properly controlled, it can become as deadly as an economic forest fire.

The African-American community has every reason to be on the front lines in this battle for our nation's economic soul. Black unemployment has skyrocketed to levels that haven't been seen since Michael Jackson released *Thriller*. Nearly half of all black children are living below the poverty line. Black wealth has continued to shrink, as the burst of the real estate bubble left many African Americans either homeless or upside down in their mortgages. Black families have been destroyed by the prison industrial complex, where Wall Street firms earn billions each year from slave labor. Also, several Wall Street banks deliberately targeted black and brown communities for predatory loans that put grandma out of the house she'd lived in since Malcolm X was alive.

Yes, we have reason to be very, very upset. It is in part because my grandmother was one of the people who lost her home due to predatory lending that I plan to join my brothers and sisters (of all races) in their decision to occupy Wall Street. This is our chance to confront the economic bullies who've worked to politically castrate nearly every politician in Washington, and also those unpatriotic enough to allow the country to sink into the financial abyss.

I wish I could say that major civil rights organizations would join us in this fight. But I am reminded of the decision by the NAACP to take millions of dollars from Wells Fargo, a bank accused of predatory lending. This is not to say that they won't join the battle, but it does say that biting the hand that feeds you isn't exactly the key to economic prosperity. This might be a lesson to all of us that in spite of the fact that we all need money to survive, we must be careful about making ourselves dependent upon a resource that is controlled by the descendants of our historical oppressors.

No matter how you slice it, the Occupy Wall Street movement belongs to the people. By seizing the moment and putting it all on the line, we have an opportunity to help fulfill the long-lost dream of Dr. Martin Luther King Jr. If Dr. King were alive today, he wouldn't be asking Washington bureaucrats to give him a multi-million dollar monument funded by corporate America. Instead, he'd be right down on Wall Street with the protesters, demanding justice, freedom and equality for the American people. In fact, if you look into the eyes of those who've become inspired to resurrect the spirit of conscientious activism in America, you can see that Dr. King's spirit is down on Wall Street right now.

Kids Must Be Forced to Hear Uncomfortable Messages

Someone told me today that in order to connect to young people, I can't go bashing violent, destructive rappers, many of whom have become their heroes. They said that by speaking plainly about the horrible messages that our kids consume everyday, I might alienate those kids who've become convinced that men like Lil Wayne (who has been locked up more times than I can count, and honestly may be dying) are their true role models. I said this to my friend:

1) I'm not bashing rappers, because I love most of them. I love hip hop more than any other genre of music, and I didn't even start listening to music until hip hop hit the scene. Rappers are also my brothers, and I show my love by encouraging them to consider the power of their messages. In fact, I dare say that I study the most ratchet music out there, and I actually enjoy a lot of it. I don't appreciate the destructive message, but just like eating greasy, fattening food, there is a joy we get from expressing ourselves without restraints. So, rather than presenting myself as the dietitian who pretends that he hates chocolate cake, I am the guy who says, "Look, I

know you love this stuff and I love some of it too. But we have to think about what this is doing to our bodies."
The same is true for digesting toxic messages. Sure, creative expression without any consideration for social responsibility is a lot of fun. But we can't simply allow our desire for a good party to make us forget that we have rappers that are hypnotizing young kids to believe that "if a n*gga makes you mad, you need to blow his g*ddamn brains out."

2) If someone is teaching your child things that are going to put him in prison or the morgue, you are responsible for your child's demise if you choose to keep your mouth shut. I'm a parent, just like most of the people reading this message. I have to be honest and say that my kids DO NOT listen to hardly anything I say. The same hood culture that dominates the psyches of disadvantaged kids has also sunk into the brains of my own, with various degrees of impact. So, the way I keep myself calm while having those wretchedly difficult conversations is that I know that even if they go out into the world and make dumb decisions because of these negative influences, they can never say, "My father didn't warn me." Being honest, that's about all a parent can do.

My mama didn't tell me the things I WANTED to hear and neither did the father who raised me. They told me what I NEEDED to hear, and that's why I'm not writing this message from a prison cell. I didn't listen to them as much as I should have, as no kid does. But as I got older and started to realize what kind of man I wanted to be, those messages became more and more relevant with each passing day.

My note for the hard-working parents seeking to raise their kids above the BS is simple: DON'T-GIVE-UP and keep on having those difficult conversations. It's not for any of us.

Professionals Get Nailed by the "Bait" of Non-Existent Opportunity

I once knew a famous rapper. We don't talk much anymore since all of the booty and bling have distracted him. But that's beside the point.

A few years ago, the rapper and I were talking about women and relationships. That was when he introduced me to a concept he called, "the bait." According to my friend, he was never going to get married. He feared losing his money in a nasty divorce, didn't want anyone judging his behavior and had a general fear of commitment. But he said that sometimes, his greatest asset was the fact that many of the women he met on the road believed that they could win "the lottery ticket" and convince him to marry them.

So, rather than actually marrying anyone, my rapper friend forced dozens of women to jump through numerous hoops, s****l and otherwise. Then, he would simply throw them back into the dating pool, like a "catch and release" fisherman, giving them nothing in return for months or even years of loyalty. All they'd have to show for their efforts were a few good memories and perhaps a nasty venereal disease from all the women he'd slept with.

Rather than assessing what this man had done to their predecessors, every woman was convinced that she was different from all the rest. Many of them seemed to believe that they were the ones who could convince him to be faithful. The reason he'd dogged the other women out in the past was because they were "bad people and b*tches." Sadly enough, this man's female acquaintances honestly believed that if they were nicer, more loyal and more devoted than the last woman, she would be the one he chose above all the rest.

I see this kind of behavior in corporate America, academia and other American institutions, where sometimes, being black and outspoken is a serious crime. Some institutions, such as the Harvard Law School, which go decades without promoting more than one or two token African Americans, are not held accountable because those in a position to speak are hoping that they can receive a different outcome from the hundreds of other black people who've been rejected in the past. In the minds of some, their predecessors were not promoted because they weren't smart enough, didn't work hard enough or didn't make enough sacrifices. It never crosses anyone's mind that you might be just another n*gger, sent through the endless revolving door of broken dreams.

I admittedly feel sorry for those of us who've been convinced that if we are quiet, patient and uncritical, we will be that one negro that the blatantly racist organization decides to hire or promote. It's like being afraid to speak up against the actions of a rapist because you are hoping he will propose marriage to you. You are instead encouraged to applaud him for working to overcome his "little problem" and for the fact that he is raping far fewer women than he did in the past. But deep down in your heart, you know that someone has to stand up to the BS, you're just hoping that person doesn't have to be you.

Part of the reason I was able to create an independent scholarly career is that I analyzed the experiences of my predecessors. I knew that my employer, Syracuse University, hadn't granted tenure to any African American in my field in the entire century of operating history. Not to say that I didn't think I could be the "chosen Negro" and get the promotion that was denied to scores of scholars before me, but I wasn't willing to give up soul, my integrity and everything else in order to find out. I'd seen those before me give everything for a reward that didn't exist, with many of them ending up angry, disillusioned, and sometimes even insane.

I figured out very early that there are some who would view me as a criminal for simply being an intelligent and honest black man. I knew that by simply pointing to uncomfortable, yet undeniable facts about historical racism, I would be labeled as the same trouble-making, radical black boy that my teachers considered me to be in the fifth grade. I also knew that you can't go into someone else's house and expect to move around the furniture. When you don't have the power to get your own food, you have only earned the right to sit your black a*s down quietly and say "thank you" for the scraps that you've been given.

After sacrificing to create my own platforms and engaging in scholarship outside the oppressive walls of academia, I've run into an odd fascination from other scholars. They either admire me, are jealous of me, don't understand me or fear the consequences of being associated with me. Many of them want the recognition, power and wealth that comes from speaking to a broad audience without the sacrifices and risks necessary in order to get there.

I don't judge my brothers and sisters who've made different choices, I simply feel sorry for some of them. I speak at corporations and universities regularly, where folks will pull me into the corner and give me a long description of the racism that they've endured at the hands of their superiors. I don't always know what to say, because the fundamental truth is that when we ignore Malcolm X's lessons on self-sufficiency, you then have no choice but to politely accept the constraints of your situation.

The bottom line is that many of us, scholars included, must consider alternative paradigms of success and economic progress. When we judge our achievements based on the accolades that have been bestowed upon us by institutions that were designed and built for others to succeed, we are at risk of believing that everything we've worked for is worthless. Many of us end up frustrated, devalued and unsuccessful, in large part, because we've agreed to play someone else's game on a field that was designed for them to win. The secret to failure in America is to spend your whole life seeking validation from the descendants of your historical oppressors.

What's also true is that equality and power are never granted freely. Therefore, by seeking meaningful and honest progress in the struggle against racial inequality, you sometimes end up going head-to-head against those who benefit readily from the inequality against which you are fighting. It's hard to imagine anyone speaking up against a harmful bully with no protection, and then expecting the bully to reward him.

To make a long story short, thinking outside the box is necessary for us to reach our individual and collective goals. Martin Luther King and Malcolm X both used teachings from across the world to inspire national progress on civil rights. No matter how smart we are, or how educated we become, the reality is that education in the absence of courage or independent thinking is going to lead us right back to our respective plantations. This, my friends, is a fact, even for the "chosen Negroes" among us.

The Racial Wealth Gap Is a Festering, Untreated Disease

A new study presented some disturbing, yet expected news about the sad state of economic affairs within the African American community. According to the study, the wealth gap between white and black Americans has become the widest that it's been in the last 25 years. As it stands, whites have a wealth level that is 20 times greater than blacks, and 18 times greater than Hispanics.

Much of the drop in black family wealth is due primarily to the decline in home values and heightened unemployment during the great recession of the last three years. African Americans currently have the highest unemployment rates in America, with the most recent data listing the rate at 16.2 percent.

The wealth gap is the largest that it's been since officials began tracking the disparities back in 1984. At that time, the gap was merely 12-to-1, implying that African Americans are worse off than they were in the 1980s, when Ronald Reagan promoted trickle-down economics, which destroyed black communities everywhere.

"I am afraid that this pushes us back to what the Kerner Commission characterized as 'two societies, separate and unequal,'" said Roderick Harrison, a former chief of racial statistics at the Census Bureau. "The great difference is that the second society has now become both black and Hispanic."

Another reason that whites are so much better off than blacks is because they are more likely to own stocks. The same Wall Street bankers who caused the recession were the first to be bailed out, leading to a quick recovery for those who owned securities. Whites are far more likely than blacks to own 401(k) and IRA plans, in addition to stock funds, with these assets accounting for 28 percent of their wealth. On the contrary, only 19 percent of black wealth comes from these assets.

Each time I notice how much worse off the black community has been during the last three years, my mind goes back to the statement by President Obama, in which he argued that the "rising tide will lift all boats" as it pertains to the economic recovery. The argument by the Obama administration was that by dealing with the broader economy, African Americans would naturally benefit. At the time, there were those who expressed concern, given that this policy of ignoring economic inequality sounded a lot like a racialized version of trickle-down economics.

Since that time, black unemployment has risen by 150 basis points (14.7 percent to 16.2 percent), while white unemployment has declined (9.4 percent to 9.1 percent). Additionally, black family wealth has dropped to levels we haven't seen since I was a little boy. Having so many Wall Street bankers on the Obama administration economic team doesn't add much hope that perhaps our government even remotely understands the complexities of deep and historic wealth gaps between blacks and whites in America.

Like a festering disease left untreated, racial inequality has resurfaced in America. Most interesting is that nearly every member of Congress and the Obama administration has remained tone deaf to the issue, arguing that there are bigger fish to fry than the uncomfortable issue of race. The differences in composition of black wealth vs. white wealth clearly implies that different economic medicine must be used for different segments of our economy. One cannot always treat two different illnesses in two different sections of the body with the same medication. Trickle-down economics didn't work in the 1980s and it is not working today.

The Republicans will surely jump on this information, arguing that African Americans have little reason to support President Obama. The problem they have is that history clearly proves that they won't do any better. Their opposition to Affirmative Action programs, opposition to labor unions and desire to hammer Social Security, in addition to their commitment to ruthless and uncompassionate capitalism, implies that they would only worsen the wealth gap themselves. Their hero, Ronald Reagan, is the one who sent our nation into the tailspin of deficit spending and greed that puts our nation on the brink of its first default in history.

At the same time, the Democrats expect African Americans to line up in lockstep with every issue that matters to them, but refuse to say a peep about the intense and persistent economic pain within black America. As a result, we have a black president who grants our community tremendous symbolism, but refuses to take a stand on racial issues because he knows that white liberals won't like him anymore. As a result, he fills his cabinet with elitist Harvard cronies and Chicago political colleagues whose only interest is preserving power and manipulating our minds to ensure his reelection.

The evidence clearly shows, without question, that black people are not better off under Obama. It is up to the Obama administration to provide evidence to the contrary, rather than hoping that their political foot soldiers will discredit anyone who speaks up on the issue. The rising tide is NOT lifting all boats, so we need a better solution than that.

Dear Academia: Stop Telling Me that Black Boys Are Not Important

This week, I sat on a Congressional Black Caucus panel for the Janks Morton film "Hoodwinked," starring myself, along with Marc Lamont Hill, Jawanza Kunjufu, Steve Perry and Ivory Toldson. One of the men on the panel was Dr. Bryant Marks of Morehouse College, a highly-respected scholar who focuses on the success of African American males in his research.

Professor Marks and I had a brief conversation before the panel about the state of black males in America. One of the other parties in the conversation was John Wilson, the head of President Obama's initiative on HBCUs. John is a likeable person, and it is my greatest hope that all he said about the president's commitment to HBCUs was real talk and not just political spin. Others, such as Professor Darrell Issa, who claims he might be sent to prison by Joe Biden's son for a peaceful protest at Delaware State, seem to have concerns about the future of our Historically Black Colleges and Universities.

I envy Dr. Marks, for he has the great honor of educating black men at the greatest generator of black male achievement in the history of the United States.

Morehouse College is second-to-none when it comes to helping our men stake claim to their greatness, humanity and personal power. You can always tell a Morehouse man when you see one, for he has been built to be a special breed. Unlike many black students at predominantly white institutions, the Morehouse man is not made to believe that he has to overcome second-class citizenship in order to be respected as a human being. In many cases, he is built for leadership.

After speaking about a visit to Morehouse, Dr. Marks and I also talked about the fact that many black scholars feel that they almost have to apologize for doing research that focuses on black men. At white universities, you are typically told that this kind of work is not of significant scholarly importance or that you're being too narrowly focused in a world that seems determined to believe that is has become sufficiently post-racial. Black men have the highest unemployment, incarceration and homicide rates in the nation, and we are expected to act as if everything is normal. To h**l with that—our families cannot survive if our future heads of households are having their futures murdered in broad daylight.

One of the reasons I fought so much with my colleagues at Syracuse University is because I was told that my advocacy for black men made me something less of a legitimate scholar than my colleagues. If I was on CNN talking about black males, there would be no mention of it, even though my colleagues would get accolades for appearing in the local news. Of course it was easy to ignore the criticism, since I was trained by some of the best scholars in the world in my field and I was determined to bring my expertise back to my community. Also, the fact that my business school has not tenured one single black finance professor in over 100 years of its existence speaks to the awesome wall of blinding racial inequality that had been built over several decades. In other words, racism makes people stupid.

Dr. Marks and I came to the same conclusion when it comes to studying black men: Our boys and men are important and we don’t have to apologize for a d**n thing. We are the husbands, fathers and leaders of our community, and it is critical that we do all we can as scholars to build and equip as many black intellectual warriors as we possibly can. I see brilliant black men in all walks of life, who’ve been convinced that their intelligence should be used to bust rhymes, throw a football or convert grams to ounces. So, our unharnessed power is everywhere, and all black parents, scholars and mentors are called to the front lines in the battle to save our children.

Also, black women are a critical part of this fight as well. Mothers are often the first teachers of a child, and also a woman's ability to find an adequate husband is largely determined by whether we raise our boys to be responsible men or a pack of reckless "baby daddies." As Frederick Douglass once said, "It's easier to build strong boys than to repair broken men." So, the protection of our cultural ecosystem is highly contingent upon all of us being committed to raising our children to be strong, responsible, intelligent and productive. We are all in this game together.

Black Unemployment Rises To Rates Nearly as High As the Great Depression

The Bureau of Labor Statistics released the unemployment data for the month of December, and while things are getting better for whites, African Americans continue to suffer from unemployment rates that would be unimaginable if those being affected were of any other race. White unemployment rose slightly from 6.8 percent to 6.9 percent, with white males seeing a decline from 6.4 to 6.2. White women saw a slight bump from 6.2 to 6.3 percent as well. These numbers are mildly uncomfortable, but have led to a tremendous backlash from those who feel that this is evidence that the Obama Administration has not been entirely effective in securing sustained economic growth.

While white Americans are enjoying single digit unemployment (and still angry about it), black Americans are experiencing unemployment rates that are nearly as high as they were during the Great Depression. Black unemployment rose from 12.9 percent to an astonishing 14 percent. Black male unemployment is highest between the genders, at 14 percent, while black women are grappling with a 12.2 percent unemployment rate. Black teens are getting the worst of it, with an unemployment rate of 40.5 percent, nearly double that of white teens (21.6).

The numbers continue to beg the question of whether or not legislators and the Obama Administration should be expected to utilize targeted economic policy that accepts the reality that there are racial disparities in employment opportunities in America. While the Democratic Party scoured the nation going into every black church and community organization they could find to get us to vote, they are ignoring these very same institutions when their members call for some kind of help with the unemployment crisis which exists in black America. Billionaire Bob Johnson, among others, has openly stated that when it comes to black unemployment proposals presented to the White House, the officials agree that the proposals are a good idea and then never agree to do any follow-up. What if black America never agreed to follow-up with the Democrats when they came begging for our votes?

One problem for the Obama Administration is that they seem to think that racism simply doesn't exist, at least that is what is implied through their actions. They, like some other Americans, seem to be thoroughly convinced that black people don't have jobs because we don't want to work, or that we don't care about feeding our children. But this is contradicted by stories like the one about the unemployed woman who pretended to be white and found that the number of job interviews she received suddenly skyrocketed.

I know people with Ph.D.s and law degrees who struggle to keep employment, so the myth of the lazy negro who doesn't want to work needs to be squashed in exchange for policy recommendations that respect our rights to equality as members of the American family. I'm sorry people, but Al Sharpton and Ben Jealous aren't going to be able to convince the Obama Administration to do the right thing: They will personally benefit from having access to the White House, but the rest of us do not. As it stands right now, the old adage of "taxation without representation" is an excellent way to describe the state of affairs in black America. Our taxpayer dollars are being taken so we can help white women get jobs and to pay for Al Sharpton to have a show on MSNBC.

Memo to the White House: Racism is real, and we need your support. You have hundreds of billions of dollars in taxpayer resources at your disposal, much of that drawn from the black community, and it is required that you utilize some of those resources for targeted economic policy which calls for the support of black-owned businesses and economic support to urban areas that are hardest hit by the unemployment epidemic. If white Americans have the right to scream and complain about a "wonderful" unemployment rate of 6.9 percent (which black people won't even have after our recession is over), then black people certainly have the right to be outraged about 14 percent. Any other perception of the situation is nothing less than entirely racist.

Black Entrepreneurship is Key to Solving Problems in Black Unemployment and the Black Family

I recently traveled to New York for a panel on black male fatherhood, hosted by former NBA player Etan Thomas. The panel consisted of other great athletes, including former NY Knick Allan Houston, Billy Hunter (Executive Director of the NBA Player's Association), Chris Broussard from ESPN and several others. One of the topics that came up was economic security as a contributing factor to the breakdown of the black family in America.

This issue burns me up because some of us don't see the link between black unemployment, mass incarceration and the breakdown of the family. When men can't get jobs and a chunk of them are in and out of prison, the numbers of men eligible to run a household decreases dramatically. So, even though some of us don't care about these issues, the reality is that these problems affect all of us.

The black unemployment problem is one of the leading economic crises to hit the presidency of Barack Obama. It is also the one that the administration has probably ignored the most. This economic elephant in the middle of the room is both a problem that politicians consider unnecessary and too difficult to solve. It is mostly unnecessary because Obama and his team have always known that they never had to deal with the issue in order to keep black loyalty. It is difficult to resolve because the reasons for the problem run incredibly deep.

Writing for *TheRoot.com*, Keli Goff does a wonderful job of highlighting the importance of developing black businesses as a way to fight the black unemployment problem. She mentions that minority employers are far more likely to hire black people, so black-owned businesses can be open lots of doors to the rest of us. This evidence is further shown by the recent story about the woman who changed her race from black to white on Monster.com and then received dozens of additional job offers.

Here's the deal: People tend to hire those with whom they have the most in common, those who they understand and those with whom they feel most comfortable. Unfortunately, we're usually not included in that group. This is doubly true for black men, who find that merely being intelligent and confident can lead others to treat you like a criminal. Therefore, it is not surprising that black male unemployment is the highest for any other group in the country. The bottom line is that when we choose not to shuck and jive at every turn, we can easily be perceived as being a threat.

Things cannot continue this way if we are seeking to rebuild the black family in America. We must also stop buying into systems that only serve to perpetuate our own oppression. One of the ways to get off the economic plantation is to ensure that all of us and our children learn the basics of starting our own businesses. You don't have to be a full-time entrepreneur, but everyone should at least develop a part-time revenue stream. This additional economic security will not only improve your ability to provide for others, it also frees you from the shackles of having to remain quiet and loyal in the face of blatant disrespect from others.

The Obama Administration can help matters by providing more funding to support and develop black businesses. Targeting government resources to the areas that are hardest hit by the recession could make a difference. While he's at it, the president can lift his pen and start putting together task forces to re-examine prison sentences for Americans who received harsh terms for drug distribution 10 and 20 years ago. We all agree that those sentences were long and Draconian, and we also agree that most of them tended to be handed down to black people.

Rebuilding the black family in America is going to require us to think differently and try new strategies. The advantage of being where we are is that we know for sure that the old models aren't going to work. So, in order to secure our individual and collective economic security, it's time that we learn to start owning our own stuff.

Thoughts about Sending Your Kids (or Yourself) to College and Dealing with the Cost

In the last few years, the cost of college has gotten out of control and student loan debt has skyrocketed along with it. Outstanding student loan balances have risen to $956 billion, which is a 4.6% increase over the previous quarter. Also notable is that student loan debt, unlike credit card debt and mortgages, cannot be discharged in the event of a bankruptcy.

The government is arguably doing a good thing by increasing the availability of student loans. But increased availability of these loans leads to rapid increases in university spending, largely because many students can afford to pay a tuition bill that might not have been affordable otherwise. The same thing happened in the housing market just a few years ago since increased availability of financing is an easy path to inflation.

I went to college myself and left school with more debt than some small countries. I don't regret the loans because my education is the most valuable asset I own (I went to school for 12 years after I finished high school, and it made me a better, more determined man). At the same time, I can think of ways I might have been able to keep the costs down. So, here are a few tips to parents and students on how to get educated without breaking your financial back for the next 20 years:

1) **Do you have to attend a private or out of state university?** I argue that the answer is "no." Knowledge is pretty much the same, whether you're getting it from an elite private school or a community college. What does vary, however, are the quality of the students and the quality of the connections you have after graduation. One of my kids attended Columbia University in New York on an athletic scholarship and she has doors opened to her that she might not have had otherwise. But if the university does not have a name that will give you a huge advantage in the job market, you might be better off sending yourself or your child to the flagship university in your home state.

2) **Don't be afraid of debt if necessary:** Most of the greatest companies in history were founded with debt. Debt is not a horrible thing by itself. Actually, it's the irresponsible use of debt that gets people into trouble. The worst thing I've ever seen is a person passing up on the chance to go to college because they don't want to owe any money. This means that rather than seeing an

increase in compensation and quality of life that can be used to repay the debt, the person would rather be poor, uneducated and debt free. That never made much sense to me.

3) **Let your kids pay at least some of their own loans**: If you're a parent over the age of 40, you're going to be retiring soon. Even worse, you're going to need a lot of money to maintain the lifestyle to which you are becoming accustomed. Your child, on the other hand, will be hitting his/her peak earning years right when you're headed to your financial sunset. Does it really make sense that you're paying their student loans? No, it does not.

Not only does it lighten your load to allow your child to take on some of the financial burden, it might make him/her appreciate their education more. College students should not only have a full load of classes, but I also recommend them getting a part-time job. Working not only fills up idle time that might be spent next to a beer bottle, it also builds character, time management skills and a sense of responsibility. Don't morph your child into a welfare recipient, give them a chance to grow up.

4) **Online classes can be better than going back to school:** The greatest university in the history of the world is called Google.com. I encourage everyone to use it. When I want to learn something new, I don't sign up for a physical class. Instead, I find an online class on the topic, Google the concept repeatedly, or pay $10 to learn about the topic from one of the many experts on Youtube. Universities are no longer a necessity when you're seeking to expand your base of knowledge. If you're trying to get a new skill on the other hand, there are several online classes that can give you certifications you might be seeking out.

Nearly everyone should go to college or at least learn some kind of marketable skill. But the goal of education should be at least three fold: 1) To gain a skill that you can use to make a living, 2) To become an intellectually liberated human being and 3) To find your way to financial, spiritual and psychological independence.

So, if you're only learning in order to work for someone else, then you're already designing yourself to be a high paid slave. The lack of ability to think freely or determine the source of true economic independence only makes you a cog in the wheel of a capitalist machine of oppression.

Even some of the highest paid people I know hate their jobs and hate their lives, in large part because they were never trained to seek out an existence that is more meaningful than the kind of car you drive.

That empty feeling you have every night while sitting in your living room might be your true destiny calling you from an alternative universe. Education (not just going to school) gives you the ability to know the difference and also helps you to determine the path you are destined to travel. Don't let a little debt, or fear, keep you on the sidelines. Teach your children to do the same.

Let's Also Discuss Black Youth in the National Conversation on Bullying

A football coach in Chicago has been arrested for arranging the beating of a student. Cassius Chambers of Fenger High School has turned himself in to police and been charged with simple assault. The charges were brought forth after Chambers allegedly helped over 20 football players come to the home of 16-year-old Darion Jones, where they proceeded to beat him mercilessly right in front of his mother.

Jones had been accused of stealing Nike flip flops, and another assistant coach for the team watched it all go down without doing anything to intervene. In the fight, Jones' prosthetic eye was damaged and his tooth was knocked out. Fenger High School is also notorious for the beating death of 16-year-old Derrion Albert in 2009.

When I read about this beating, my stomach turned. I'm not sure if Darion stole the flip flops or not, but the idea that this kind of vigilante justice was endorsed by members of the coaching staff is beyond shameful. The incident speaks to the fact that

Fenger, as well as other schools around the country, are unable to provide adequate protection for young black children who are regular targets of this form of bullying. Scores of black children die in Chicago every year, yet there is very little national discussion of these tragedies.

In South Central Los Angeles, thousands of youth grow up with Post Traumatic Stress Disorder after wondering if their walk to school is going to be interrupted by an AK-47. All the while, most of the conversation about bullying tends to focus on gay kids in the suburbs. Yes, all plights are worthy of discussion, but one has to wonder if black youth were factored into our nation's sudden decision to begin discussing this problem (I don't recall seeing any black kids on the AC360 discussion on bullying, nor have I seen the issue of urban bullying featured on any national media outlet).

It must be made clear that Darion and millions of other children in urban communities across America are regular victims of a type of bullying that is rarely seen in the suburbs. His mother has already lost a child to gun violence, and the fact that we've come to accept this as a normal part of "growing up in the hood" should sadden us all.

The national discussion on bullying should bring forth specific conversations and action plans for children in urban communities, so that they can feel as safe as the middle class kids whose coaches DON'T arrange for them to be beaten in front of their moms.

The kids in the suburbs don't have gun shops and liquor stores on every corner, conjoined with massive unemployment and low educational quality to accelerate the chances that they might find themselves being beaten or shot by a bully who's not even in school anymore. A well-known example might be the scene in the famous film, *Boyz in the Hood*, where one of the teen characters is murdered in an alley after getting into an altercation with a 27-year-old man. This story is played out repeatedly all over the country, yet some seem to believe that for young black men in America, dying is simply a part of life.

Kids like Darion Jones need help. They need our protection and they need to feel safe. Additionally, getting rid of the guns, improving educational quality and reducing the massive black teen unemployment rate (regularly over 40 percent) might be a step in the right direction. So, not only should bullies be confronted for their behavior, we should also stop turning urban neighborhoods into "bully incubators" that create the destructive characters who end up slaughtering and traumatizing our children.

For every Darion Jones whose story makes the national news, there are a thousand other black youth whose stories are never told. Many of these kids are left with the difficult choice of being judged by 12 members of a jury or being carried by six pallbearers at their own funeral. We must give good kids better options, better policies, and examples to show them that their lives are just as valuable as the kids who have a little money. Being picked on is obviously depressing, sad and hurtful, but our kids are the ones who are being regularly beaten and shot.

Five Reasons Why Financial Education is More Important than S*x Education in Public Schools

Two things that tend to affect our brains in the same way are money and sex. They are also two things that can get us into the most trouble. So, as a Finance Professor, I thought I would explain five reasons why financial education is at least as important as, if not more important than, sex education and why both should be taught in high school.

1) **Because it's relevant:** We teach our kids the birds and the bees (sometimes), have them reading old English textbooks that they don't understand and force them to learn
at least 5,000 things that they will never use for the rest of their lives. If we are teaching all of this semi-worthless nonsense, why not teach a child to balance a check book too?

2) **Because we think about both nearly every single day for the rest of our adult life:** I bet you that you've thought about sex at least 20 times today and thought about money at least 10. Unless you're broke or celibate then it might be the reverse.

3) **Because they relate to one another in more ways than you can imagine:** A man who doesn't have his money right isn't exactly going to be in good standing with his significant other. When I wrote the book, "Financial Lovemaking," I recall interviewing dozens of women and being absolutely fascinated by how many of them would talk about their husband's financial inadequacies more than anything else. It was almost as if they'd rather have him cheat with another woman, just as long as the bills were paid.

4) **Because both of them open the door for us to get screwed by other people:** The easiest way to ruin your life is to let an important part of your life be controlled by an irresponsible person—that goes for both your and your bank account. I can't tell you how many emails I've received from people who've been financially devastated by their relationship choices. You don't want to join that club.

5) **Because managing both in an intelligent way can lead to a tremendous amount of bliss:** There's nothing better than being able to say, "I've got plenty of money in my bank account, and my sex life is outstanding." In fact,

the status of your bank account might impact your sex life, but that's neither here nor there.

Either way, the management of your money and your personal life can impact your happiness in more ways than one, so it might make sense for our kids to be fully educated on both. Black kids in particular need to be taught a) how to save, b) how to own things, c) how to earn money from multiple sources, and d) the importance of education in protecting their financial future.

Genius: Black Boys Over-Represented as Chess Masters

Black males are disproportionately represented in nearly every stereotype known to man. They lead the nation in incarceration, unemployment and drop-out rates. But another area where black boys are over-represented is among the number of chess masters in the United States, reminding us of the tremendous genius of young black men when placed in motivational environments.

Less than two percent of the members of the United States Chess Federation are masters. There are 47,000 members in all. Only 13 of those masers are under the age of 14. Three of these 13 masters are African American young men.

All three of the men live in New York City: Justus Williams, Joshua Colas and James Black Jr. All of them were actually named masters before their 13th birthdays.

> "Masters don't happen every day, and African-American masters who are 12 never happen," Maurice Ashley, a grandmaster told *The New York Times*. "To have three young players do what they have done is something of an amazing curiosity.

> You normally wouldn't get something like that in any city of any race.

Daaim Shabazz, a professor at Florida A&M University, keeps a website that records the number of African American chess masters in the United States. According to his site, 85 masters are African American. Justus was the first boy to meet the standards to become a master, with Joshua and James following later. "I think of Justus, me and Josh as pioneers for African-American kids who want to take up chess," James said.

The story of these young men (who are not related), is a firm example of the potential of all black boys when given an opportunity to succeed. A little encouragement and a chance to break the chains of problematic stereotypes has allowed these young men to become intellectual Michael Jordans. Unfortunately, too many black boys are led to believe that their genius starts and ends on the football field or basketball court, but the truth is that the greatness we show in sports can be replicated in all walks of life.

I recall simply applying techniques I'd learned from playing sports to propel me in my quest for academic achievement. I haven't looked back ever since.

Teacher Calling Black Students "Future Convicts" Reminds Us of What's Wrong with Education

Jennifer O'Brien, a teacher in Paterson, New Jersey is in serious trouble after some remarks she made about her first graders on Facebook. The teacher, who'd grown frustrated with her class, went on Facebook and stated that some of her students were "future criminals." The bulk of O'Brien's students are black and hispanic. During her peculiar Facebook post, O'Brien stated that she'd just spent another day in the "blackboard jungle." She then went on to say "I'm not a teacher, I'm a warden for future criminals."

Later in the day, O'Brien went back to Facebook to ask why her first graders couldn't be put into a scared straight program, which allows young people to meet real prison inmates. "They had a scared straight program in school—why couldn't I bring 1st graders?" she said.

O'Brien's comments got back to the school board, who suspended her immediately. This week, she appeared before a government school inquisition, who asked her about the situation. That's when O'Brien told an administrative judge that she wrote the post because six or seven students kept disrupting her lessons and interrupting the children who wanted to learn. O'Brien claims that one boy hit her, another one hit a child in the class, and that she had filed several disciplinary reports with the principal.

> "I was speaking out of frustration to their behavior, just that build up of 'I don't know what else to do,' and I'm actually scared for their futures, for some of them," O'Brien said. "If you're hitting your teacher at 6 or 7 years old, that's not a good path.
> "
>
> "The reason why she was suspended was because the incident created serious problems at the school that impeded the functioning of the building," board president Theodore Best said to *North Jersey.com*. "You can't simply fire someone for what they have on a Facebook page; but if that spills over and affects the classroom then you can take action."

While O'Brien's frustration is certainly understandable, it's not difficult to see that her comments are rooted in the same racial bias that destroys so many black and brown children in America's broken school system. Although Ms. O'Brien would like to believe that these six-year-old children have already routed themselves to prison, the truth is that she herself has incarcerated her kids in the prison of low expectations. Instead of spending her time trying to elevate their minds to become doctors, lawyers and professors, Ms. O'Brien seems to believe that the most she can do for her six-year-olds is keep them out of jail.

I find myself personally disappointed with O'Brien's remarks because I was one of "those" children: Horrible grades, in detention more than class, and in the principal's office so much that I knew the names of his wife and kids. The truth was that I wasn't a dumb child or one who was destined for the penitentiary; I was looking for a teacher who gave a damn about me and didn't think I was a menace to society. And to be honest, school bored me to death because no one ever explained how a good education could help me make more money (which matters quite a bit to kids who are born to single mothers in the projects).

If Ms. O'Brien can't handle little black kids, she doesn't need to be teaching them. The school district in Paterson would be wise to realize that there are thousands of highly-qualified black and brown teachers, consultants and counselors who know how to handle black children. Unfortunately, the overseers of our educational systems would rather have the black/brown inner city children poisoned by the white female teacher from the suburbs than to have that child exposed to someone like myself or Dr. Marc Lamont Hill at Columbia University (you know, those controversial and "dangerous" black men). So, in some ways, even as adults, many of us are still being treated like the children in Ms. O'Brien's class—"at risk black boys"—a simply label that translates into "dangerous black men" when we enter adulthood.

I recall visiting an inner city school in my hometown of Syracuse. The school was 70% black and latino, yet every single teacher in the seventh grade was a white woman from the suburbs. The school was depressing both inside and out, like a cross between a penitentiary and an insane asylum. I was asked to speak to the children with alleged learning and behavioral disorders. It was interesting to see the shock on the faces of the teachers when they saw how well their black male students responded to another black male: They were quiet, respectful, and many of them came to me afterward asking what they should study in college. This outcome was in stark contrast to what their baffled teachers claim they'd seen from the students every other day.

The reality is that educating black and brown kids is not rocket science. But trying to educate them without sufficient cultural competence is like running a nuclear reactor with a manager from Burger King. Our children have a tremendous amount of potential, but unfortunately, their futures are aborted before they even have a chance to exist. The American school system is probably one of the worst places in the world for black kids to be educated, and superiors to women like Ms. O'Brien should have a zero tolerance policy for such immature and short-sighted behavior.

There is no such thing as a six-year-old convict. We must find a way to give that child a chance.

What Malcolm and Martin Would Say About the Black Unemployment Problem

Hello everyone,

In case you aren't aware, there continue to be disturbing trends in the unemployment data. You may have heard in the media that the unemployment numbers last month were optimistic, but that was not true for the African American community. According to data from the Bureau of Labor Statistics, unemployment declined for every demographic within the white community, but it actually increased for every measured group within the African American community (men, women and teenagers). Even worse is the fact that after this recession is over, black unemployment won't be any better than white unemployment is right now (Racial Inequality 101). As you can read in this article, I am perpetually united with other black scholars and public figures who are deeply concerned about this issue.

Many years ago, Malcolm X and Dr. Martin Luther King shared their visions for the African American community. Dr. King's dream has been co-opted and morphed into a message that has become both shallow and commercialized, while Malcolm's dream was forgotten altogether. Both of these men told us long ago that black unemployment would continue to be a chronic economic disease for our nation until African Americans find ways to own some of the businesses that are giving out jobs. But after spending 400 years having our wealth extracted, thus killing our ability to pass anything onto our children, we continue to find ourselves economically marginalized.

To help alleviate these issues, we've put together two initiatives. The first is the Ujamaa Initiative to support black businesses. I have agreed to serve as the national spokesperson for the Ujamaa Initiative, which has the sole objective of bringing together black businesses with consumers wishing to support them. We must find ways to strengthen the businesses in our communities instead of begging for jobs that will never come to pass.

The second initiative we've put together is the "Less Talk, More Action Empowerment Tour," which I've joined with financial experts Ryan Mack and Manyell Akinfe, along with Columbia University Education Professor Christopher Emdin and Entrepreneurship guru Andrew Morrison. The tour is designed to travel the United States to offer substantive, tangible solutions to economic problems that continue to plague the black community. We address three key issues that continue to be ignored by politicians clamoring for our votes: Educational inequality, Economic inequality and Mass Incarceration. All three of these issues work together as (what I refer to as) the Holy Trinity of Racial Oppression and continue to decimate the black family in America. The Your Black World Coalition, which now has 76,000 members nation-wide, is committed to finding solutions to these problems.

Our goal is to embrace black scholarship in action—you won't see us hiding away in our offices writing research papers that only a few dozen people are going to read – we take our knowledge and expertise to the people where it belongs.

Until we meet again, stay strong, be blessed and be educated.

PurposefulParents.com: Old-Fashioned, Down-Home Advice on How to Make Sure Your Kids Know How to Read

Ms. Robin from *PurposefulParents.com* talks about ways that you can ensure that your child knows how to read. Ms. Robin has been married for 38 years, and has three children: A doctor, a college professor and an Ivy League graduate. She has also been employed as a counselor in the public school system for over 25 years. Ms. Robin gives very simple, straight-forward advice on how you can ensure that your child is ready for their future by making sure that he/she knows how to read. Her bottom line: Don't wait on the school system to do it for you.

Hi, I'm Dr. Boyce Watkins from YourBlackWorld.com and one of the things we do here at Your Black World is that we have a segment called Purposeful Parents and part of the reason that we have this segment is because we believe that parenting is something that is done well when it is not done by accident. Being a great parent is not something that you do just because you gave birth to a child it's something that you do because you commit yourselves to doing a very good job.

One of our regular contributors to Purposeful Parents is Ms Robin, and I have Ms Robin on the line and she wants to talk about making sure your child can read and not relying on the educational system to teach your child to read.

Boyce: Ms Robin, how are you today?

Robin: I'm fine how are you Dr. Boyce?

Boyce: Doing very well, very well. Now you are—you are a Southern Woman; you've been married almost 40 years; you are a strong Christian woman and you raised your kids to be pretty successful and so I'd like to turn to you to get advice on what we need to do with our kids. I'm down in Florida right now with the National Alliance for Black School Educators and one of the things that we talked about at dinner was not just what needs to happen when our kids are in the classroom but also what needs to happen in the home. You happen to work in the school system, but you are also a mother and a wife; you have struggled with some of the challenges and you felt pretty adamant about this idea of not relying on the school system to make sure your child can read. Can you talk to us a little about that?

Robin: You should start educating your children as soon as they come into the world. It's important that parents read to their children daily but once the kids start school, you'll want to make sure that they can read yourself. You want to verify what the services are that you're thinking you're getting from the school system. For example: When a first grader comes home from school every day, you want to review the alphabet or whatever it is that she's learning, her spelling words. Make sure that she's actually learning what the school tells you that she is learning. Also have your children read out loud to you and it's very important that they read out loud. That way you know what level of reading that they are at.

Boyce: Ok, so you're saying that it's not enough, as a parent, to just send your child to school and make sure that they have good grades—I've seen this myself, with my own kids. Sometimes you might think that your child is getting what they need but actually they're not. You're saying that it's really up to us as parents to make sure that our an kids are getting that, that they're actually doing something that is constructive for them in terms of reading. Am I hearing you correctly?

Robin: Yeah, absolutely. Use the public school system as a source for educating in school but you supplement it; you can supplement with getting outside tutoring services that may be available in the community. If you can afford to pay for someone else to tutor your child—just to verify that your child is learning exactly what they need to learn—then do so. I'll give you an example. My youngest child had some issues where the teacher was telling me that he wasn't functioning in school and he wasn't performing at the level that she felt like he should be performing. She made the assumption that he did not know how to do it. So we paid a tutor that specialized in tutoring African American boys and I would take him to the tutor once a week and she was verifying that what the teacher was saying to me was actually true.

Boyce: Hmm, interesting ok. Just so people know. There are a lot of families that may not necessarily have a lot of money to afford extra help and things like that. Is this something that somebody even on a modest income would be able to afford? What would you say if someone said, "Hey I want to help my child, but I don't have a lot of money." What suggestions might you offer to a parent like that?

Robin: Well, first of all, there are usually many churches that have after school tutoring programs. So you could look at your local church. Even if you don't attend church, you can haul around to some of the churches in your community to see if they offer after school tutoring programs. And then also, if you can't afford tutoring, look at your budget and the money that you may be spending on tennis shoes, cell-phones, and other things that you could cut back on or sacrifice such as cable TV, movies, and things that we typically spend money on and; instead, spend it on tutoring. But there are lots of free tutoring programs. Some of the schools even have after school tutoring programs.

Boyce: Ok, so what you are basically saying is that when you look around and you see people who are spending money on going out and buying a flat screen TV, they're really spending money on things that they don't need that we also want to make sure we invest in the things that we do need when it comes to getting our kids what they need. Am I right about that?

Robin: Absolutely! You'll find out that a return on your investment—in making sure that your child can read—is going to be a lot greater than that flat screen TV that you probably won't have in 10 years.

Boyce: Well, hopefully we'll have our kids for more than 10 years.

Robin: The child is going to go into adulthood either reading or not reading—that's my point.

Boyce: Ok, that's a good point. I'll tell you raising a child who can't read is a very bad investment because then that child will be after you for money for the rest of their lives. So I tend to agree with you on that. I want to say thank you so much Ms. Robin. Ms Robin is one of our leading contributors for *Purposeful Parents.com* and she is part of our army of parents who are determined to make sure that our children are getting what they need and that they become who we want them to become or who they're capable of becoming. So I want to say thank you so much for your time Ms. Robin.

Robin: Thank you very much.

Boyce: Thank you and thank you all for checking us out at Your Black World.com and until we meet again please stay

strong, be blessed and be educated. We are gone.......
Peace.

15-Year Old Starts Tech Company, He's Now a Millionaire

Jaylen Bledsoe is a one-of-kind superstar. The 15-year old sophomore started his own tech company a few years ago, and has found entrepreneurship to be his calling. As a result, he is his own man, and a millionaire because of it.

Jaylen says that he started his firm when he was 12-years old, and plans to attend Harvard after he finishes high school. Jaylen's company, Bledsoe Technologies, is now worth an estimated $3.5 million. This means that if he manages his wealth in the right way, he will be set for life.

Jaylen doesn't spend his time memorizing lyrics from the rapper "2Chainz," smoking weed or chasing girls on Saturday nights. Instead, he spends his time chasing paper, pursuing his dreams and positioning himself for a truly empowered existence.

Personally, I'm proud of him. I can also see that he is the beneficiary of good parents and role models. Our kids are like products off an assembly line: The outcomes we see in kids Jaylen's age are direct products of what they've been exposed to on a daily basis. It's just as easy to manufacture a businessman as it is to manufacture a thug.

Jaylen's company does web design and other forms of IT consulting for companies located mainly in the Midwest. He actually reminds me of another young person I met recently, Emerson Spartz, the founder of Spartz Media. Spartz is not African American, but both of these young men serve as powerful templates for what our boys can become if given the right guidance.

When I spoke with Emerson, we both agreed that around the age of 12, we probably had ADHD. But we also both agreed that, while ADHD gets you in trouble in school, it can actually be beneficial to have a mind that races from one good idea to the next. Personally, my short attention span caused me to struggle in school until I gained my footing in college. High school felt like prison to me, and my horrible grades reflected that sentiment.

Emerson's parents had a better idea: Take him out of the school system altogether. But not only were they going to home school their son, they also decided that they weren't going to force him to learn any particular subject. Instead, Emerson's parents focused on making sure that their child could read well, communicate in writing, and do math, which is pretty much what any person needs to know in order to succeed in life. I've rarely seen anyone struggle in their profession because they've never read old English literature or learned the Periodic Table in Chemistry.

So, basically, Emerson's parents allowed him to study whatever he wanted, which sounds almost insane. They also required him to read a biography of a successful person every day to get a vision for his future. Before long, Emerson, like a lot of kids, gained a strong interest in Harry Potter. He then went on to found Mugglenet.com, the largest Harry Potter site in the world. So, just like Jaylen, Emerson was a 15-year old millionaire. He is now a 26-year old genius with a natural and burning desire to learn new things. He's been featured in *Inc Magazine* and was a *New York Times* best-selling author by the age of 19. Speaking to him was like talking to other college professors in academia.

Young men like Jaylen and Emerson define the vision of what we're seeking to do with the group of educators we've gathered around the country for our homeschooling initiative at Your Black World. The public school system is failing our children miserably, especially black boys, turning potential leaders into tiny men with low self-esteem. This has produced a state of emergency where, for every Jaylen Bledsoe, we produce a thousand wannabe rappers, basketball players, and prison inmates. I must be entirely honest when I say that the next Martin Luther King is having his future aborted every single day of the week.

Public school systems have become a virus, infecting millions of our boys with the disease of complacent mediocrity. With each additional day of education, they become more deeply socialized into the mental health crisis that undermines their ability to become strong husbands and fathers. They then enter into an economic system that is not wired to give them employment, even when they've made good choices and obtained several years of post-secondary education; as a result, black men have the highest rates of unemployment, incarceration and homicide in the entire country. Let's face it: This nation is not designed for most black men to be successful and a thousand marches on Washington will never change that.

My suggestion on this issue is simple: 1) Every black child in America should be home schooled, even if they go to school someplace else, and 2) Every black child in America should be taught the basics of how to run their own business.

Homeschooling may not mean taking your child out of school every day, but it does mean using the time that your child is not in school to teach him skills he will need to be a successful adult: The basics of black history, how to be a good parent, how to buy a home, etc. In other words, it means being a truly educated human being with adequate life skills and the ability to engage in critical thinking. Critical thinking can make the difference between life and death, or poverty and prosperity: Nearly every black man runs into a George Zimmerman at some point in his life, whether it's a white racist trying to harm him or another black man trying to put him in the grave. Critical thinking protects us from dangers we deal with every single day.

Secondly, being an entrepreneur doesn't mean not working for anyone else, but it does mean having alternative streams of revenue so that you are not enslaved by a corporation that causes you to check your freedom and self-esteem at the door. That way, when situations call for you to stand up, you're not faced with a corporate overseer telling you to sit right back down. Living paycheck-to-paycheck, deep in debt, on one stream of income is a surefire pathway to a lifetime of socioeconomic servitude.

Our youth must be prepared to survive and compete in a world that doesn't always love them, and have the skills necessary to overcome obstacles that they will most likely face in their path.

We MUST create more Jaylen Bledsoes and fewer Lil Waynes. The truth is that both of these young men are geniuses, and both of them know how to work hard. The difference is that one of these men is a net asset to his community and the other is a blatant liability. One of these men is positioned for freedom and the other has been pre-assigned to psychological slavery. One of them is going to live long and prosper, while the other one might be dead before the age of 35. Both of these men are prototypes, and every prototype can be replicated with the thoughtful design of pre-determined structural and environmental factors.

Don't believe me? Check out Rosz Akins and the Carter G. Woodson Academy in Kentucky, where she empowers and educates extraordinary young black men who are equipped to become world leaders in politics, business, science and everything else. This DOES NOT happen by accident.

America incarcerates more black men on a per capita basis than South Africa did during the height of apartheid. In this country, a prison cell and a casket are being built for every black boy on the day he is born. If we do not change the trajectory of that child's life at an early age, then their fate is already sealed. Not only do our boys have the tools to survive all enemies foreign and domestic, they have the power to thrive and conquer when their energies are channeled in the right direction. Our community MUST regain control of this process, and we must not take "no" for an answer.

In the words of Dr. Christopher Emdin, *we must occupy our children.*

Five Things College Students Do to Ruin Their Lives

As a college professor for the past 16 years, I've noticed two things about college: It can be a place to make your dreams come true, and it can also be a breeding ground for your worst nightmares. So, I thought I would compile a list of things that I've seen college students do to ruin their lives over the years. Hopefully, you and your child can learn from what I am about to share.

1) **s*x, drugs, alcohol and gambling**

College is a great place to pick up a lot of really bad habits. The worst part is that people tell you that these things are ok. It's not that all of these are bad things to do, but at the very least, they should be done in moderation. It doesn't matter if you are in college: If you have s*x with too many people, you are going to catch a disease or get pregnant. If you use drugs, you are going to become a drug addict. If you drink too much, you will become an alcoholic. Gambling can also ruin your life as much as drugs or alcohol. I have several dozen friends with really messed up lives to this day, all of whom started their downward spiral on a college campus. You should not think that because you are in college, you are immune to these problems. If something doesn't feel right, then you shouldn't do it. Be mature enough to make smart decisions.

2) **Falling for the credit card scams and ruining your credit**

There are no serious credit card scams in college, only the little people who stand out in front of the bookstore trying to get you to take their "free money". Credit cards are very tempting when you are in school, especially since you are broke. If you decide to take one, make sure that you are very careful with how much you buy with the card, and that you have a careful plan to pay it all back. Putting yourself in over your head can easily destroy your credit. That is not a good cycle to get into. Not taking care of your student loan obligations can ruin your credit as well. You should manage your debt as best you can, because if you don't, it can take decades to fix the problems that are created.

3) **Working too much outside of school and forcing yourself to drop out**

Getting a job in school is not a bad thing to do. In fact, it builds character. But you should work only to support your basic needs. If you find yourself working non-stop in order to pay for things that you shouldn't be buying in college, then that is when it is time for you to settle down and reconsider your priorities. Your professors are not going to care if your grades are in the toilet because you are engaged in too many outside activities. It is your responsibility to keep up in class. You will have the rest of your life to work, make money and buy all the things that you want. If you do it all too early, you are going to kill your chance to ever have the finer things in life. My mother used to say to me that "People who work hard before they are 24 get to party hard when they are 30." I didn't understand that then, but when I was 31 years old bringing in the New Year on a cruise ship in the Bahamas, I understood what she meant.

Additionally, the temptation to leave school for "just a little while" may seem to make sense, but it doesn't. Most Americans never graduated from college, but most of us went to college for at least a while. For many college drop outs, the distraction may have seemed temporary at the time, but turned out to be quite permanent. Don't get off the educational track, because the hurdles of the real world can be very deceptive.

4) **s******g up their freshman year**

There are a ton of students out there who are spending every waking moment of their sophomore, junior and senior years trying to compensate for the massive mistakes made during their freshman year. If you get off to a bad start, you're asking for serious trouble all through college. You will have to do 10 miles of work to get 5 miles of reward. Don't put yourself in that position if you can avoid it. The best way to avoid problems in the freshman year is to use a consistent study strategy. That means, you should set aside at least 5 hours per day in which you go to a secluded spot in the library and stay there. Make sure that no one else is around. You can do whatever you want for the rest of the day, but make sure that your studies get their proper attention. After you've put in your class and study time, you will have a good 5 or 6 hours a day to have all the fun you want, especially on the weekends (remember: there are 168 hours in a week. If you are in class for 15 hours, sleep for 56 and study for 42, you still have about 55 hours left for parties! That's a lot of party time!)

5) **Pledging a fraternity or sorority too early**

The quickest way to ruin your GPA and put yourself on a downward spiral in college is to pledge a fraternity or sorority during your freshman year. Some frats and sororities are responsible enough to make sure that they don't allow freshmen to pledge. But even if they are not a freshman, you should not allow yourself to pledge until you've had a good academic year. If you are still struggling academically after your freshman year, you should wait and pledge the grad chapter. You will have the rest of your life to be part of the group, and you can still go to the parties and have lots of fun without being in the organization. I never pledged, but I had friends in every fraternity. The difference was that I didn't have an obligation to anyone, but I had respect for people in all the different Greek organizations.

Education matters more than almost anything you'll ever do you in life. If you blow the opportunity over foolishness, you'll spend the rest of your life regretting it.

Chapter 4

Mass Incarceration, The Black Family and Intergenerational Pain

Rev. Jesse Jackson Says that Jails are Financially Exploiting Families of the Incarcerated

This week in an article in the *Chicago Sun-Times*, Rev. Jesse Jackson spoke about the mass incarceration epidemic that is harming families all across America. Millions of children grow up in psychological turmoil because the head of household has been sent to prison for dozens of years, in many cases due to non-violent, drug-related offenses. Not only does this process serve to create more criminals (which happens to many children who grow up with a missing and incarcerated parent), it also leads to corporations using the families of incarcerated Americans are a way to fuel their bottom lines. One of the forms of exploitation that Rev. Jackson notes is the high cost of making a phone call in the Cook County Jail.

In Cook County jails, prisoners are charged as much as $15 a call to be in touch with their relatives. The exploitive rates can force families—already struggling with the burdens of having a loved one locked up—to choose between supporting their loved one or paying for heat or food. An Illinois study found that the price of phone calls from prison was one of the two most significant barriers to family contact during incarceration.

Since when should it ever cost anyone $15 to make a phone call? I make calls from my cell phone for pennies. Even I would have trouble paying such a high rate at my own income level. If most of us would struggle with this cost, why would we expect a poor family to be able to pay the price? Even if you care nothing for the inmates themselves, should the children and relatives of this person be forced to give up nearly everything just to speak to the person they love?

Rev. Jackson gives insights into why he believes that inmates' families are attacked with this horrible financial burden:

> "Why are the most captive and vulnerable being charged such brutal rates for a phone call? Because they can be. They have no choice in provider. The prison system cuts a deal with a telephone company that pays the state a "commission" — what the *New York Times* calls a "legalized kickback" — that ranges from 15 to 60 percent of the revenue. Thus, as a report by the Prison Policy Initiative details, state prison systems have no incentive to select the company with the lowest rates. Instead, the correctional departments gain the most by selecting

> the company that provides the highest commissions."

The result makes prison-telephone use a cash cow for the phone companies—and a brutal exploitation of the families of prisoners who pay the charges. Not surprisingly, over the past few years, three corporations have come to monopolize the service of 90 percent of all incarcerated persons, making it even easier to control rates.

Rev. Jackson continues to make a very good case regarding why we should reconsider these legalized kickbacks and see them for what they really are: A serious form of economic corruption that leans on the tendency of our society to care nothing for poor, black and brown families. The mentality for many is that if you are arrested for a crime, you deserve no legal rights or human rights, even for a petty offense. We also seem to forget that people of color are arrested and incarcerated more regularly than whites, even when they commit the same crimes. Also, in states like Illinois, patterns of police torture have been consistently unearthed, showing that many of the individuals in prison didn't do anything at all.

Rev. Jackson states that such policies actually increase the rate of recidivism, making our society more dangerous for all of us:

> "These outrageous rates make it harder for prisoners and their families to stay in touch. Yet studies show that family contact and support is directly related to the success of a prisoner after release. As the Prison Policy Initiative reports, the 2012 Republican Party Platform endorses "family friendly policies . . . [to] reduce the rate of recidivism, thus reducing the enormous fiscal and social costs of incarceration." The 2012 Democratic Party Platform also supports initiatives to reduce recidivism. A sensible step would be to lower prison telephone rates."

According to Rev. Jackson, rates for prison phone calls vary throughout the nation. In some states, the rates are as low as five cents per minute. In others, they can be as high as $17 per minute. What's made abundantly clear is that there are ways to manage the expensive kickback corruption to ensure that the punishment fits the crime. Torturing the families of inmates should not be part of the incarceration package in America.

Rep. Bobby Rush from Illinois and Rep. Henry Waxman from California are asking that the FCC act on this matter (I encourage you to consider supporting them). It is also imperative that our nation revisit the devastating impact that the failed War on Drugs has had on our society. America cannot succeed by incarcerating such a large percentage of the population for minor, non-violent crimes and then decimating the families of the convicted. It's not good policy and it is up to our political leadership to address the issue in a fair and ethical way.

Former DEA Agent Says He Was Told to Only Lock Up Black People for Drugs

Matthew Fogg, a former U.S. Marshal and Drug Enforcement Agent, speaks candidly in a video about his experience in the War on Drugs. Fogg says that he noticed that most of the drug raids that he set up were in urban areas, typically targeting people of color. Fogg said that most of the members of his team were white, which led him to ask the question that might only be asked by the black guy in the room:"Why aren't we setting up raids in the suburban areas too?"

Fogg notes that African Americans aren't the only ones using and selling drugs, yet most of us notice that the prisons are full of African Americans, the bulk of them there for drug distribution. He says that he was told to "stand down" on the matter and informed that doing drug raids in white neighborhoods would lead to political consequences for the agencies involved. He even said that the team would "lose their overtime."

I appreciate the courage that Mr. Fogg showed by speaking so honestly on the issue. My father was a law enforcement official for 25 years, and I've heard similar stories myself. Also, as a college professor over the last 20 years, I can say that the amount of drug use on college campuses rivals nearly any urban neighborhood in America. In spite of this, I have yet to see the police raid any fraternity house on a Saturday night. So, for every person who believes that black men are filling the penitentiaries because we are the only ones committing crimes, you might want to get an education on the matter.

President Obama, are you listening? I hope that Congress is listening too, or any political figures who've received more than 80% of the African American vote. The War on Drugs has decimated the black family in America, leaving millions of children to grow up without their parents, all due to a set of federal policies that have been proven time and time again to be as racially-biased as those implemented during the Jim Crow era. It's time to confront these policies, and make things right.

President Obama, as well as any Democrat on Capitol Hill who spent six months begging black people to stand in line for hours in order to vote, needs to do some or all the following (thanks to Political Science Professor Dr. Wilmer Leon for making these recommendations):

1) Call for a review of all cases in which individuals were sentenced under the old federal guidelines and re-sentence them accordingly. I've heard from families of men who've received over 14 life sentences for first time, non-violent drug distribution. This amounts to torture.

2) The president should form a federal task force to determine how many people have been affected by the old standards and make recommendations on how to correct the wrongs of the past.

3) President Obama must use his bully pulpit to speak on mass incarceration and the impact of the prison industrial complex, even noting the well-documented racial disparity. I know that President Obama might be afraid to tell America that he's a black man, but it's time to let the cat out of the bag.

4) The president should ask the Attorney General to form a task force to provide recommendations on how to address this issue. From what I know about Eric Holder, he wants to do this. I encourage him to provide strong leadership on an issue that affects so many men like himself, even if Valerie Jarrett tells him not to.

Fogg's story is a disgusting reminder of how many of those arrested for drug crimes are political prisoners. Black women today have difficulty finding husbands because so many men are in prison. Black children are missing critical mentors, and our community is falling apart at the seams for the numbers of men and women who've been hammered by the holocaust of mass incarceration. It's one thing to make drug arrests, but when those policies so blatantly impact one segment of the population, we should all be outraged.

Study: Black Male Incarcerations Jumped 500% from 1986 to 2004, Resulting in a Mental Health Crisis

A report has been released at Meharry Medical College School of Medicine about the devastating impact that mass incarceration has on our society. The study, published in *Frontiers in Psychology*, is one of the most thorough examinations of the impact that mass incarceration has on the African American community. The study's authors argue that the billions of dollars being spent keeping non-violent offenders behind bars would be better spent on education and rehabilitation. According to Dr. William D Richie, Assistant Professor in the Department of Psychiatry and Behavioral Sciences at Meharry Medical College and lead author of the paper:

> "Instead of getting health care and education from civil society, African American males are being funneled into the prison system. Much of this costly practice could be avoided in the long-term by transferring funds away from prisons and into education."

The study's authors note that 60% of all incarcerations are due to non-violent, drug-related crimes. The authors also note that the cost of substance abuse in the United States is as high as half a trillion dollars per year. "Spending money on prevention and intervention of substance abuse treatment programs will yield better results than spending on correctional facilities," the authors claim in the study.

Finally, the authors note that while crime rates have declined over the last 20 years, incarceration rates has climbed through the roof. The inmates occupying these jail cells are disproportionately black. In fact, the black male incarceration rate has jumped by 500% between 1986 the 2004. The authors note that, even for those who don't abuse drugs before going to prison, the likelihood of substance abuse after prison goes up dramatically.

The mass incarceration epidemic affects all of us, even those who haven't gone to prison: It affects the child who grows up without a father who has been incarcerated, the children who are bullied at school by that child, the woman seeking a husband who can't find a good man to marry, the list goes on and on. When so many of our men are marginalized and incarcerated, this has a powerful impact on the sociological ecosystem of the black community, the same way an economy crumbles when a few large companies go bankrupt.

The point here is that we cannot look at the holocaust of mass incarceration as someone else's problem or something that just affects criminals. The punishment should fit the crime, and when every study imaginable says that black people are more likely to go to jail for the same crimes, this means that Jim Crow is alive and well. Something must be done at the grassroots, state and federal levels. We cannot allow this epidemic to exist any longer.

Why Being Educated Can Sometimes Cause You Pain

I spoke with a formerly incarcerated man recently who told me about his experiences inside the state penitentiary. I could instantly tell that this man was brilliant, as smart as any college professor I know. He recited legal statutes, laid out subtleties of American politics, and spoke about entrepreneurship as if he were an expert.

The man had used his 20 years in prison in the most productive way possible, learning everything he could. He also seemed to feel that he had a lot of catching up to do, now that he was a free man. He explained a few things about his experience, like how surprised he was to find that in most maximum security sections of the prison, black and hispanic men fill up nearly every cell. He said that most of the white guys he saw in prison were in the low-security and safer sections of the prison (surely to protect them from the "scary" black men). His story reminded me of my experience in public school where black boys landed in the special education classes (they tried to put me in those classes too), and the college prep classes were filled with white kids. The educational and prison systems are inherently the same and like the NCAA to the NFL, one has become a feeder into the other.

The man also said something that really made me think. He reflected on how he'd gone to prison as a young drug dealer, receiving an incredibly harsh sentence for a non-violent crime. He also mentioned how painful it was to get his education in prison and become enlightened on just how imbalanced the criminal justice system is when it comes to young black men. He said that learning about the circumstances of his incarceration both infuriated him and raised his blood pressure because his awareness came at a time when he was not the least bit empowered to do very much about it.

I tried to understand the man's pain as much as I could, even though I've never gone to prison myself. My biological father went to prison for drug possession and my older brother figure (technically my uncle) went to prison as well. So, while I'd seen the devastation of incarceration up close in multiple sections of my life, I was fortunate enough to avoid the traps that were set to destroy me. But what I could certainly relate to is the fact that sometimes, ignorance can be blissful because the more you understand what others are trying to do to you, the angrier you can become. At that point, you gain the stigma of being the angry black man standing in the middle of a bunch of drunken, happy Negroes.

I encourage everyone to educate themselves as much as possible, I must warn you that the more you understand, the more frustration there is to uncover, particularly when we discover truths about what this country did to our ancestors on its way to stripping us of everything we had. That's why black kids in public school aren't given access to accurate and honest depictions of American history and are instead fed drugs, liquor and Lil Wayne albums. They want you to be the smiling, ignorant Negro, not the angry black man, even if you have legitimate reason for being angry.

No one is ever going to voluntarily give your intellectual freedom. That's something that you're going to have to take.

Why Our Kids Have the Right to be Outraged

A young woman in Chicago was seen on video cussing at her teacher for refusing to teach the kids in class. The young woman was passionate, angry and fed up with not getting what she deserved. In this interview, Dr. Boyce Watkins and Maria Lloyd discuss how we might process situations where students express this form of outrage and whether or not it's justified. The transcript of the interview is below.

Dr. Watkins: Hi I'm Dr. Boyce Watkins from the YourBlackWorld.com. Some of you may have seen a video that has been circulating all throughout the Internet. In the video, there was a young woman who was in a classroom and for whatever reason, this young girl was fed up. She was angry that the teacher would not teach her. She yelled and screamed and said, "I'm tired of you not teaching us. I'm tired of you telling us stupid stories. I'm tired of you telling us about smoking weed." I think she said something like that, I'm not sure, but basically the girl was just tired of hearing things that had nothing to do with her education and I was inspired by the video because I love seeing young people stand up to get what they deserve and also it is ironic that she's from Chicago which is a city that has so many problems when it comes to our youth—whether it's violence, a poor educational system, or the lack of economic opportunity, etc.. To discuss this, I want to bring you one of our editors at Your Black World, Ms. Maria Lloyd. Maria happens lives in Chicago, so she has an inside point of view on this. Maria how are you today?

Maria: I'm doing well, how are you?

Dr. Watkins: I'm doing really well, really well. Can you describe how you felt when you watched this video and some of the thoughts that went through your head?

Maria: Absolutely. Well, first off, my heart is shattered because I think it's pitiful that we have to have our youth stand up for education, demanding education, and we are not demanding that on their behalf. So, my initial response was literally, my heart was shattered. I had tears in my eyes when I watched this child stand up with conviction and basically just exude the frustration that we should all have that our kids are not receiving the resources they need to learn, and you know, better themselves.

Dr. Watkins: You know I felt the same way. I wrote an article about it and I said you know this anger this girl is showing, it's something that maybe all of us need to show. I actually quoted Laurel Thatcher Aldrich, a Harvard professor who said, "Great women are rarely well behaved." So, everybody who watched this video and looked at this little girl and said, "Oh! She's not a, you know, a well-behaved child. She needs to be more disciplined. She needs to sit down." Well guess what? When it comes to doing what's right, you have to be willing to misbehave. Now, again I'm not assuming that I know the whole story, I'm not assuming that this teacher was a bad teacher or even that this woman had a reason to do what she did. But let's go ahead and try to make that assumption that there was a legitimate concern that she was expressing in the classroom. Well, maybe she was right to stand up and say this is enough, you know, enough of this nonsense. If you look at some of the greatest people in this country, one of the greatest individuals in America actually lives in Chicago in the south side, Father Michael Pfleger one of the things that people know about Pfleger. One of the things people know about him is that he misbehaves on a regular basis because his approach to life is "What would Jesus do?" and Jesus would misbehave if it comes to doing what's right. So, when it comes to doing what's right for our families, for our children, and for our communities, we have to be willing to misbehave. We have to be willing to stand up and speak up and I'm in alignment with you. I think it's atrocious that these kids have to stand up for their own education and the adults won't do anything. We have the adults just sitting back and just observing and watching and wagging our fingers and saying, "What's wrong with these kids?"

You see what's going on in Chicago, which is all around you—you live right there in the heart of the south side. You have family members in the south side. You see what's going on with incarceration affecting our families. You see what our children are growing up with. What do you think people need to understand about some of the challenges that young ladies like this girl might be going through—that might help us to understand where she's coming from?

Maria: The thing I want people to understand about these kids is that they come from a home where they probably don't know their father; the first words they learned were profanity; they learn how to fist fight before they learn how to read and their mothers have left them home alone for days at a time. They have friends who are in gangs. They've witnessed their first murders when they were just small children and they've probably been abused by their mother's boyfriends. So in other words, we have kids who have gone through trauma that is as horrific as the soldiers are going through in Iraq but; yet, we expect them to grow up and be productive citizens. And I think, until we can understand that these kids have not been fostered in a loving, caring environment, we will never be able to help them because they are not getting the love that they need from home. So, are we going to sit back and continue to condemn these kids and look at them and say, "Look at this idiot Chief Keef. This man is a fool?"

That man, that child, has probably never ever in his life ever had an adult tell him, "Good job. I love you. You are amazing." These kids have never been encouraged to do anything. So, when we have a young lady like this who's standing up and asking for education. She's not asking for welfare. She's not asking for any handout. She's asking for an education, a quality education. We should not sit back and condemn a child for asking for something that will make them a productive citizen in this country. So, we have to first understand that these kids have not received the upbringing that they need and it's not their fault. It's our fault for allowing them to grow up in these environments and not take them under our wing. As you always say Dr. Walkins, you don't have to have a child to be a parent and that's very true. We don't have to have children to be a parent to these kids.

Dr. Watkins: I love it and I think that's so true. We have to remember the value of the village when it comes to raising our kids and when that child is in your life. Just because you're not the sperm donor does not mean that you don't have the obligation and opportunity to impact that child's life. Remember that when you impact the life of one child, you're impacting the lives of all the people that child is going to interact with over their lifetime. So, if you allow a child to grow up with hate and neglect in their heart, to the point where they become a monster and a menace to society and hurting other people, well, part of that blood is on our hands for allowing that child to become the faulty individual that he or she might become after growing up with that kind of neglect. I think about that every time I think about a guy who murdered a three year old. I thought, well, when this kid shot this baby, when this kid was a baby himself, nobody loved him. So, as a result, he grew up and became a monster. So, we got to stop creating monsters in our community by allowing these children to be neglected and based on what I saw, I stand by this young lady. I say speak up, scream up, to the black leaders of our country as far as I'm concerned and that's exactly what we need. We need somebody to put some fire under our butts and convince all of us to stand up and do what's right. So, I'm very happy that she did what she did and I think that was one of the greatest displays of passion that I've seen in quite a while. So, thank you very much for your time Maria. I really appreciate it.

Maria: Thank you.

Dr. Watkins: And thank you all for checking us out at YourBlackWorld.com, and until we meet again please stay strong and be blessed and be educated. We are gone. Peace.

Chapter 5

The Death of Black Boys and Girls: Black on Black Crime, White Supremacy and The Police State in Urban America

The Gift of Trayvon Martin – His Sacrifice Has Awakened a Nation

Most of us will never forget how we felt on the night of "the verdict." This was the moment where all of black America shed the same tear, and our worlds became a little darker than they were the day before. We were having racism thrown right in our faces, with a justice system that said, "We're going to exterminate your children and trample your human rights and there isn't a d*amn thing you can do about it."

The pain was sharp and intense for all of us. What's interesting to me is that it's not as if the world suddenly changed on the night that George Zimmerman went free. It's that many of us suddenly realized what the world already was. All of the so-called "Racial Chicken Littles" who'd been yelling about injustice for years, suddenly had the ears of everyone, including middle class black folks who'd come to believe that if we are well-behaved, hard-working and law-abiding, then everything would be ok.

The truth is that America has always been racist and corrupt. Finding out about racism on the night of the George Zimmerman verdict is like the doctor telling you that you have cancer when it's been eating away at your body for years. The disease of racism has crippled America since our nation was founded, and the sickness has festered because we don't have the courage or ability to treat it. Rather than responding to racism proactively, intelligently and courageously, we've behaved like the sick, yet arrogant patient who thinks everyone else is ill and that he's extraordinarily healthy.

America incarcerates more black men than South Africa did during the height of apartheid, yet we somehow consider the country of South Africa to have been worse off than us. Just as many African Americans have lost their lives from the War on Drugs as there were Jews killed during the N*azi holocaust, yet we somehow disconnect the names Adolf Hitler and Ronald Reagan.

The Trayvon Martin/George Zimmerman trial was a human alarm clock, awakening a beast of ferocity that hasn't existed in black America since Angela Davis was a college student. Black people across the board are fed up with a corrupt criminal justice system that has created more criminals than it has rehabilitated. We are sick of school systems that make our kids less intelligent than they were when they arrived. We are tired of an economic system that thinks black people should silently enjoy depression-level rates of unemployment.

I won't even talk about the violence, where many of our kids can't even walk to middle school without wondering if they are going to die the same way as their classmates. Suburban kids are worried about their math test. Inner city kids are dodging bullets delivered by gun manufacturers who profit by mass producing black g******e.

Trayvon's gift to the world is that he gave enough of a shock to our system that we're all wide awake, angry and not going to take it anymore. Polite debates on Fox News are nearly turning into fist fights. Office conversations with that well-intended bigot down the hall might end up with someone getting fired. There is almost no tolerance for anyone who somehow justifies how a deranged, gun-toting lunatic can profile an unarmed child and be acquitted after killing him like a dog in the street.

There is almost no room for forgiveness, at least not this time.

Trayvon has given his life in a manner that has become a blessing to all of us. His painful and untimely sacrifice will have a ripple effect that lasts for at least a half century. Black America has been changed forever, and I truly believe that, when the dust has settled, we will be stronger than ever before. As I said earlier, the beast has been awakened.

White Man Kills Black Teen Over Loud Music

Florida is ground central for suspicious shootings of young black men. Just a few months after the shooting of Trayvon Martin, a teenager in central Florida has also been shot under suspicious circumstances. Michael David Dunn shot and killed Jordan Russell Davis, a student at Samuel W. Wolfson High School.

The 17-year old was sitting in an SUV in a parking lot when Dunn came up and asked him to turn his music down. The two exchanged words, and that's when Dunn shot at the young man eight or nine times, killing him in the process. His attorney says that the shooting was in self-defense.

Russell's father, Ron Davis, says that his son died in the arms of one of his friends. He also says that he was unarmed. Dunn has been arrested and charged with both murder and attempted murder. He is being held without bail.

The fact that Dunn plans to say that the shooting was in self-defense brings the controversial "Stand Your Ground" law back into the spotlight. But what is also sad is that while many African Americans will be up in arms over this shooting, almost no one says a word when black men shoot one another. This happens in nearly every major city, every single day of the year. It seems that black death only gets attention when it's done by someone of another race.

KY Man Shot in the Neck, Killed in Racially-Disturbing Case

Police in the state of Kentucky are trying to find out what happened to a man who was fatally shot in the neck in the town of Raywick, Kentucky. The incident is disturbing because the club in which the shooting took placed has been dogged with allegations of racism.

David Litsey of Lebanon, Kentucky was shot and killed outside the Raywick Bar and Grill early Friday morning. Litsey was shot in the neck while allegedly trying to break up a fight, and some are saying that he may have been shot by one of the club's employees. Litsey, a father of three, died on his way to Springview Hospital.

Sheriff Jimmy Clements said this is the first homicide that the town has seen in years. An employee at the bar said that Thursday nights tend to get wild, and that several fights broke out.

No arrests have been made, but a relative of Litsey's, Tiffany Adams, reached out to me to give her side of the story and ask for a deeper investigation. Here is what she had to say:

> "My cousin's nephew went to neighboring Raywick on Thursday night to a bar formally known as Susie's Bottom Up. In the summer there was lots of controversy with this club not allowing black people entrance simply because they were black. As a matter of fact there was a video on YouTube from one of the nights were someone recorded the bouncers saying the owner said no blacks allowed."

Raywick has a LONG history of racism. There is only one black person who resides there and has for years. David Litsey was 22yr old father of 3. He went to this bar where a fight broke out and he by many eyewitness accounts, he assisted in breaking the fight up. He reportedly entered the club to get his other friend so they could leave and a bouncer there assumed he was instigating a fight and fatally shot David in the neck.

His friends put him in the car trying to stop the bleeding and drive quickly to Lebanon trying to make it to Springview Hospital, the only hospital there. He died before they made it there and it's only a 10 minute ride. WHAS 11 reported this story yesterday and there has still yet to be an arrest. Law enforcement has told the family they are waiting for a warrant but they told the media they have no suspects at this time.

I am not exactly sure about what happened here, but a deeper investigation is certainly warranted. The state of Kentucky is one that has a very disconcerting racial history, and it's important that outside authorities investigate in order to see what happened here. Of course, Your Black World is going to look deeper into the incident to report what we find out. This is sad and shameful.

Teen Drives By His Brother's Dead Body on the Way to School: Victim of Bullying

Gun violence is the leading cause of death for young black men. One of the great frustrations for the African American community is that politicians in Washington act as if the violence doesn't exist, and our kids keep dying as a result.

The latest death was in Washington DC. Marckel Ross was killed on his way to school and his brother, Markies, actually drove by his dead body.

"I can't believe somebody would do this to him," Markies told the *Washington Post*. "He was a great person... Everybody loved him."

Marckel didn't seem to have any serious problems in his life, but he was the victim of bullying. This death was as shocking as the death of Amber Stanley, another teen in DC who was recently murdered while she slept in her bed.

While the people in Washington define the image of bullying to be someone making fun of gay kids in the suburbs, my image of an even more vicious bully is that of a 16-year old gang banger with an AK-47. As politicians look the other way while gun manufacturers grease their pockets by letting deadly weapons slip through the cracks, our kids are paying a price for our silence. Those who don't die before the age of 18 are every bit as traumatized as combat veterans, watching their friends die one-by-one.

This should not be what a childhood is all about.

Are we going to speak up for these kids? I certainly hope so. The voices should rise from the bottom to the very top, and that includes the black man in the White House who was so concerned about those dead kids in Colorado.

Poll 40% of Americans Think George Zimmerman Acted in Self-Defense

It appears that as the trial of George Zimmerman moves forward, more and more Americans are starting to believe that he should have killed Trayvon Martin. A new Rasmussen Report survey has found that only 24% of Americans believe that George Zimmerman should be found guilty of murder. Also, 40% believe that Zimmerman acted in self-defense.

The survey results are a 15% increase from the same poll conducted in March and up 16% from last month. Even more interesting is that only 47% of African American survey respondents believe that Zimmerman should be found guilty of murder, compared to 55% in March. Also, the poll claims that 40% of black respondents think Zimmerman acted in self-defense.

While Rasmussen polls have a solid reputation, it's hard to believe some of these results. Most African Americans I hear from through social media, conservative and liberal, seem adamant that George Zimmerman should be found guilty of murder. There does not appear to be much ambiguity on the African American side of things, at least no uncertainty that is being publicly expressed.

With regard to those who feel that Zimmerman acted in self-defense, it's hard to understand this conclusion when Zimmerman was clearly the initial aggressor. He had no official authority to follow Trayvon and ask him questions, and you could almost accuse him of impersonating a police officer. While Zimmerman may not have announced himself as an officer of the law, he certainly behaved like one.

Given that Trayvon was not the aggressor and he was unarmed, it's a serious stretch to argue that Zimmerman was justified in shooting him. I can't imagine myself finding a random white guy, harassing him to the point that he prepares to confront me physically, shooting him and then claiming that I was simply defending myself. If anyone was acting in self-defense, it was the frightened kid who was minding his own business and being chased by a lunatic who'd been taking medication with violent side effects.

George Zimmerman should be in prison, and he'd already be there if his victim had been white. All of this speculation about Trayvon's allegedly violent nature would not be happening if he were not a black teenager. Take it from another black man who was once a teen himself: People love assuming that we're violent.

The Day I Walked Through Airport Security Naked

One day, I was in the Denver International Airport hanging out in the non-smoking area. I had a little time before my flight, so I decided to do what anyone would do in a non-smoking area: I lit up a cigarette.

As you might expect, my puffs got the attention of overzealous airport security. Many of them obviously attended the "George Zimmerman School of Black Male Oppression," so I wasn't surprised when they asked me to put my cigarette out. But there was something about this injustice that absolutely infuriated me.

Fuming over the fact that I wasn't allowed to break the rules of the airport (after all, being Dr. Boyce Watkins should come with privileges, right?), I decided to exact my revenge. So, I "suddenly realized" that it was too hot to be wearing my Puma sweat suit and Kangol, so I stripped them right off of my body. I then realized that even my boxer shorts and socks were too much to bear, so I got rid of those too.

After a little more time spent "droppin it like it's hot," there I was, proudly displaying (what I believe to be) my most beautiful and significant body parts to the world, sporting what God gave me to anyone who happened to be passing by. I'm sure the ladies were impressed.

After stripping myself down to the "good stuff," I then noticed that I was about to miss my flight. So, holding all significant body parts in place, I sprinted butt-naked through airport security with my boarding pass and ID in my free hand. After all, I didn't want to get in trouble for forgetting my essentials.

You can imagine my shock and dismay as the terminal agents stared me down like I had a hole in my head. I was absolutely appalled by their blatant racial profiling, for I was sure that they were only coming after me because I was black. As one of the agents approached and tackled me to the floor, I started to think that perhaps I'd done something wrong.

After being tackled, I was handcuffed, humiliated and thrown in the back of a police car. I write this article as I await trial for a long list of charges, starting with some obscure FAA rule against running through the airport naked. Given our nation's shift in civil liberties since 9/11,

I'm sure that at least one of these charges comes with indefinite detention and a possible death penalty.

That's the end of my story, but before I move on, I have a confession to make: I actually made the entire thing up (yes, I can see the shock in your face). But some of this actually did happen to a woman in the Denver International airport this week. After being asked to put out her cigarette by an official, she responded in full rebellious fashion, by stripping herself nude and trying to go through airport security.

Unlike the scene I described above, the woman wasn't tackled and taken away in handcuffs. In fact, she doesn't even face charges. Instead, she was taken to the hospital for psychiatric evaluation.

"Hmmmm, very interesting," I thought. "I bet that wouldn't happen if she were a 'brotha.'"

Welcome to the world of white privilege. In this world, devious criminal activity is likely to be treated with empathy and compassion, giving the offender another chance to ruin his/her life at a later date. African Americans, on the other hand, rarely have their criminal offenses treated in the same way. Most of the juvenile offenders sentenced to life in prison without parole (nearly all of whom are Black or Latino) were victims of serious abuse before they committed their crimes. But they are rarely sentenced to simple psychiatric evaluation, and instead are sent straight to prison.

Beyond those who commit more serious crimes, anyone with experience in the justice system fully understands why African Americans have little reason to trust the courts or police. The case of Trayvon Martin, for example, is one in which even as the victim of a crime, Trayvon's family didn't receive an ounce of the respect he would have received had they been white.

White privilege must be critically assessed and challenged in all available venues. Disparities in arrests, convictions and sentencing must be taken seriously, and the system should not be allowed to continue to ruin so many black families across America. Also, sentences for drug abuse and similar activity should be treated with the same compassion that Denver police gave that naked white woman in the airport. The fact is that most of us have a story, and we can't just hear the story if the perpetrator happens to be white.

Chapter 6

What Happened to Black Love?

Dr. Boyce: Is there Something Wrong with Being a "Ride-or-Die Chick?

Sil lai Abrams, the relationship expert at *Ebony.com*, just wrote an article in which she challenged the notion of the "ride-or-die-chick." The "ride-or-die-chick" is defined, by some, to be the woman who stands by her man, no matter what. Sometimes, standing by that man might clearly lead to the woman's demise, but because she has been socialized to stick with her lover regardless, the woman is willing to go down in flames as a result.

I know "ride-or-die" women quite well. My mother stood by my father even during the toughest of times, creating a powerful rock of stability in my family that benefits me and my siblings to this day. For that, I will be eternally grateful, although I am sure that my parents' 40-year sacrifice was greater than most young people would be willing to commit to today.

Sil lai's argument is that women should not feel compelled to stand by their man at all costs, especially if the man isn't willing to do the same. On that point, we agree, somewhat. I've seen people (not just women) ruin their lives in bad relationships, and some even killed.

The "ride-or-die" topic struck a chord with me because I had a conversation last night with my daughter on that very same topic. She was asking me if a woman should stick by a man if he "has issues." Of course, as a father, my next question was, "What kind of issues are we talking about?"

Without revealing my daughter's business, I gave her this simple advice: There is nothing more precious and beautiful than a woman who has her man's back. We've become a "me first" society, where everyone seems to believe that if they aren't 100% happy and comfortable 100% of the time, then it's time to murder your relationships. Hence, the divorce rate is so d**n high that you almost believe that marriage should be banned until we all grow up and accept the fact that relationships require hard work and sacrifice. People in other countries have lasting marriages because they are willing to work through challenges that Americans would never accept.

Now, what I also told my daughter is that it's important that she be a strong, independent, observant, and intelligent black woman. I flatly stated that if the "issues" are too complex and destructive, the person should "vacate the emotional premises" immediately. I told her stories like the one about the esteemed professor at Florida A&M University who was killed by her husband in a murder-suicide, leaving her two young children without parents. At the same time, it was made clear that wearing your ego on your chest in a relationship is a great way to see it come to an end. You aren't always going to get exactly what you expect.

But the broader point to my daughter was this: Choose carefully, take your time and then stick with the choice you make. Love is not t*t-for-tat, where you only make investments in your partner because they do the same d**n thing for you. It is this lack of trust in black relationships that causes most of these relationships to fail.

Standing by your mate is more of a testament to who you are as a person than a measuring stick of what your partner has done for you. In other words, you do your job because you are an honorable human being, not because you are seeking some kind of instant emotional gratification. A woman who says, "I'll only stand by my man if I am getting what I want," is like a man saying, "I'll only be a gentleman if she sleeps with me."

Another point I am going to make to my friend Sil lai the next time we speak is that I fear living in a world where we somehow throw all gender roles out the window. Hardcore feminism sometimes seems to push the uncomfortable notion that men and women are equal and the same in every dimension, and that alluding to any type of innate gender difference is nothing short of barbaric and oppressive. But I am going to be politically correct and say this: Men and women are not the same and it's OK to accept that. Most men I know don't want to marry another guy, but when we demand sameness in every aspect of a relationship, you're effectively telling men that we should be the same as women.

Some can rightfully argue that women tend to be socially and innately built to be great nurturers and supporters (that's what makes a mother so precious and powerful in the life of a child). Many men, on the other hand, tend to be wired as protectors and providers (my mother didn't have to teach me to love football and boxing, my testosterone did it for me). So, I dread the day where every man says, "Fellas, you should only protect your woman from a mugger if she is willing to protect you in the same way," which is the corollary to what we are saying by disrespecting the "ride-or-die" chick or calling her stupid if her loyalty puts her in a bad situation. The men in Aurora, Colorado who died protecting their girlfriends from the shooter at the *Batman* movie were not stupid just because their girlfriends didn't do the same for them.

My desire to protect my significant other is not driven by some sort of instant validation or concern about whether she would protect me in the same situation. It is driven by my desire to be an honorable man, which means that I protect her because it's my job. So, rather than always saying, "I'll only do X if my partner does X," it might make more sense to say, "I'll do X because I am a decent human-being who chose a mate who is likely to do Y when I need them to do so."

The bottom line? Choose your mate wisely and then dedicate yourself to that situation without becoming addicted to immediate gratification and emotional security. Do your job because you are a good partner, not because you want them to do something for you. While the single folks might make fun of those "ride-or-die" women (and men) who stick with their mates even when they appear to be getting the short end of the stick, the truth is that their marriages tend to last, while most of our relationships do not. So, maybe there's something to be said about humbling yourself to the situation.

How Black Denial is Creating an STD Epidemic

When *NaturallyMoi.com* published an article stating that the Center for Disease Control and Prevention (CDC) said that nearly half of all black women were infected with herpes, I was intrigued by the responses that I saw. At least half of the reactions were negative attacks toward the authors for even reciting information from the CDC, as if they'd worked overtime to paint a negative portrayal of black women. It should be noted that a high infection rate among black women does not imply that black women are more promiscuous than anyone else. It might actually be the promiscuity of men that is the source of the problem (e.g. the good girl who loves bad boys and catches whatever the bad boys bring home while they're out "being bad").

I was even attacked for sharing the article on my Facebook page. Somehow, by sharing information that I felt to be a critical public health alert, I was somehow conspiring with "the man" to make black women look bad. Sorry, but I was trying to protect my daughters from a world that is designed to destroy them. I believe what the CDC has to say, because I've seen too much evidence to support the conclusions. If

we don't like what we see in the mirror, we can't get angry at the mirror, and just telling people what they want to hear doesn't lead to much progress either.
Finally, there were those who felt that the data was simply a lie.

"I don't believe this BS," some people would say. Another person mentioned that none of her five girlfriends have herpes, so the study can't be real. Someone else even felt that the data had to be inaccurate because they hadn't tested her specifically, meaning that they couldn't have tested everyone. Without insulting this person, I'd just encourage them to take a statistics class, which would help us realize why you don't have to test an entire population in order to come to a conclusion (I humbly submit that I taught math and statistics at the college level for a few years, so I've studied these methods closely). Every poll, survey or statistical analysis is based on a random sample and various tests are performed to ensure that the sample is adequate enough to get an inference on the population. The CDC has lots of good statisticians who know how to perform this exercise carefully.

So, assuming that the CDC has not conspired with the KKK to hurt black people's feelings by falsely telling us that we have an STD issue on our hands, I'd like to lay out a few reasons why we might actually have the perfect storm among us that creates the conditions for a significant STD problem:

1) **Serious and persistent denial:** I am constantly stunned by how many black people there are who simply don't want to hear bad news. They laugh when you mention that greasy food can give you heart disease. They don't want to hear you tell them that partying instead of studying is going to cause them to drop out of school. They even get angry when you suggest that perhaps Whitney Houston's decision to use drugs might have played a role in her "shocking and totally unexpected" death. Many of "us" also don't want to hear you say that there is an STD epidemic in black America. They especially don't want to hear this from a white person.

The black church is largely responsible for creating a culture of silence on STDs, since many church leaders talk about s*x as if it did not exist. The stigma of being the "good church girl" with an STD is too much for many black women to bear, so the majority of those affected won't even share this information with their closest friends. Men can be even worse, since a lot of men never get tested in the first place. So, the most horrible stories are never told and many of those affected suffer in silence, leaving the next generation to make the same mistakes because no one ever told them any better.

2) **Prison Rape:** Soooo, you think that all the men being raped in prison are being raped by STD-free men wearing condoms? Do you think that these men aren't having s*x with women when they come home? Do you think these men are going to readily tell their female partners what they were doing behind bars? Do you not think that every felon whose been entirely marginalized from job opportunities, voting rights and anything else worth living for is going to always be incredibly careful, thoughtful and disciplined in his sexuality? Keep dreaming.

The prison rape problem has long been something that people joke about at cocktail parties, but it's more serious than you might think. Not only does it constitute cruel and unusual punishment for those who've been incarcerated, it also increases the spread of STDs once the men come home and sleep with women with whom they associate.

Most men have a pretty strong appetite for s*x, and it's not uncommon for a man (especially an attractive one) to have s*x with quite a few women. Also, as a black man, I can say that many of my brothers are not very quick to go to the doctor for anything other than a missing body part. Therefore, it's not entirely inconceivable that a great deal of infection is occurring once men leave jails and prisons, especially if they do not have or choose not to utilize adequate healthcare and get full STD screenings.

This is not to put the entire STD problem on the backs of prison inmates (we already have a witch hunt in place against gay men without even considering the role that heterosexual men are playing in all of this). Instead, it's to say that the mass incarceration problem in America is one that affects the black community in more ways than one. When a man has nothing to live for and is living a dangerous life to begin with, he is not always going to take the time to protect the s****l health of women that he's sleeping with. Not all inmates are affected by these psychological maladies, but we know quite a few who are.

3) **A lack of testing:** You hear a lot of people brag about getting an HIV test, but how many people mention that they've gotten a full STD screening? You do realize that there are other diseases out there besides HIV right? In fact, many of these diseases, such as HPV, can kill both

men and women. So, you meet that really handsome guy that every other girl wants, and he makes it clear that he's not committed to you (which translates to the fact that he can do whatever he wants). You responsibly ask him his HIV status. He impresses you by showing up with a clean bill of health from his doctor, disclosing his latest negative HIV test results (assuming you wait to see the results before having s*x, which many people do not), and you take the condom off (for either oral, vaginal or a**l intercourse – a condom is supposed to be worn for all three, right?). Do you think you're completely safe? Think again.

The bottom line? There are other diseases out there besides HIV and people are catching a lot of them. Also, if you like that man, chances are that other women like him too. Finally, if he's not a man that is careful about his s****l health or buys into the BS notion that black men are supposed to sleep around, chances are that he's got a disease that even he doesn't know anything about. When my friend (a strong black man who is not part of the "CDC conspiracy") went to a barbershop and tested 20 black men for Chlamydia, he found that over half of them were infected and had no idea. Why? Because people don't get regularly tested for that disease until they start showing serious and painful symptoms.

4) **Hip Hop "playa playa" culture**: Sooo, you think that a little boy who grows up hearing Lil Wayne and other rappers measure their manhood by how many women they sleep with every year isn't going to be influenced by these messages? You don't know a single handsome man who brags about his "way with the ladies," running from house-to-house and woman-to-woman every other night? You don't think that perhaps it's possible that, the same way one man can impregnate several women, that this same man can't also infect several women too? Let's please do the math people: a man sleeping with lots of women who rarely gets a full STD screening has a very good chance of being a carrier of one of the major STDs (the same is true for women who like to "get around"). Also, any woman sleeping with him and touching his G*******a with either her mouth, a**s or v****a has a good chance at being infected. That's just a simple fact. Excuse me for not using standard Dr. Boyce language, but when people are dying, I tend to believe that honesty is the best policy—I am also equally honest with my daughters.

5) **People do not ask enough questions:** For too many men, the question of whether or not you should sleep with a woman is simple: "Is she attractive?" If the answer is "yes," then you're supposed to have s*x with her. Many women, unfortunately, have adopted the same irresponsible policy. A lot of fleeting relationships come and go without any knowledge of whose g******s were there before your own. Conversations about STD screenings and HIV status tend to dampen the mood, and that person who is "fine as hayell" brings so much pleasure into your bones that you might be tempted to believe that the things you're doing together can't possibly hurt you. This is what leads to disaster.

6) **Fewer people getting married:** I am not bible thumping and I am not saying that everyone needs to run out and get married (I've never been married myself and most marriages, quite honestly, end in divorce). I am referring to a simple fact: Most people have more s****l partners when they are single than they do when they are married (at least that's the way it's supposed to be); this is especially true for black Christian women (of course there are exceptions).

Fewer black women getting married means that single men have more pickings to fulfill their s****l desires, and women are having more relationships too. Just think about that single, 30-something girlfriend you have who always seems to have a story about relationship drama or a s****l experience she's had with a man that she's known for less than six months. In each case, she's taking on years of s****l baggage from all the women (and/or men) that this person has been with before her. But in many cases, it's "out of sight, out of mind."

7) **The imbalance between women and men:** Because of the prison industrial complex creating felons left and right, poor inner city educational systems, a lack of employment opportunities and racist media creating hoop dreams for too many black men, there is an imbalance between marriage-ready black men and women. Women grow up dreaming of becoming corporate executives or attorneys, while too many brothers grow up trying to become LeBron James. So, after his hoop dream is busted and he has no education to fall back on, many men become marginalized by society.

The imbalance between educated black men and women changes the manner by which men and women respond to one another. Many men "get around" more than they normally would because they've got so many options, and many women accept things that they might not normally consider. This creates an environment where a small number of men may end up infecting a large number of women, because the women don't halfway care whether the man is already taken or not.

For men, think about stories that "your boys" tell you about the women they've been sleeping with. Or, think about that woman who tells horror stories about the man she was with who ran through "side chicks" like they were going out of style. That's where diseases are being spread, in these short, casual relationships, as some people move from partner-to-partner, claiming to be looking for something that may not even exist. It might be fun, and I am not here to judge, but I firmly believe that you can't just do whatever you want, with whomever you want, and think that there aren't significant risks involved.

A scientist once told me that women have a psychological tendency to notice the more attractive men over the less attractive ones. This means that many men in the "attractive" category tend to be chased by all the same women. If that man has been given a license to mate as much as he wants with whomever he wants, some of these men can become walking time bombs, like the married pastor in Atlanta who was accused of sleeping with women in his church, even though he allegedly knew that he had HIV.

Perhaps it's time that we all wake up. This stuff is real. Stop believing this is a conspiracy theory and get tested....for everything. The data is accurate and there really is a problem. Ignoring this issue and not talking about it won't make it go away, and we must all make sure that we're healthy. Stop living in denial.

For the Ladies – Three Ways to Avoid s****l Tragedy

I received some resistance after writing my article about the STD epidemic occurring in black America. Some thought that by referencing the CDC study that found that half of all black women have herpes, I was somehow implying that black women are more promiscuous than everyone else. That's not the case, since another study shows that black men have four times more s*x partners in their lifetimes than black women.

I speak to my daughters on this issue all the time: You don't have to be promiscuous to catch an STD. But you can catch an STD by having s*x with a promiscuous person. Hence, the good girl who likes bad boys might have the same physical outcomes as the bad boy himself.

I heard from a woman late Friday night. She was like a lot of black women: deeply religious, raised in a single parent home, and dating a man who'd been incarcerated the year before. One of the reasons I believe we need to be consistently vocal about mass incarceration, educational inequality, unemployment inequality and the influence of commercialized hip-hop is because many of our boys are not being raised by the world to become adequate husbands and fathers. The "thuggin" bad boy might be appealing to a woman when she is 18-years old, but it can be tacky and trifling when she's 31. We have to raise our boys to be men and this demands a degree of responsibility that must be taught by both parents, even if one of those parents happens to be a surrogate.

The woman told me that after reading my article, she decided to ask her man to go to the clinic together to get tested for STDs. She said that after making her request, the man started acting strange, and refused to return her calls. I told her that this a serious red flag, and that the "goodie two-shoes" story he'd told her about not having been with anyone for over a year might not be true. Fortunately, the kicked the man to the curb after we had our conversation.

A lot of women have stories that are similar to the one that was told by the lady who called me. I encourage women to share these stories with one another, so you can learn from each other. A great example is the woman who wrote the brave open letter about sleeping with the pastor who was arrested for having unprotected s*x while he was HIV positive. Suffering in silence only allows men to run the same games over and over again. Not every man is a dog, but there are certainly dogs among us. You have to be smart to rise above the stupidity.

So, as I sit here reflecting on life, I thought I'd share a bit of "fatherly brainstorming" to help women who are in situations similar to the one described by the woman who reached out to me. Maybe you're not dating a brother who is fresh out of jail (not that these men should be condemned, but the prison rape epidemic creates obvious concern about s****l health in our community), but there is a chance that you're dating a brother, and men can be fickle sometimes. Here are three things you might want to keep in mind while playing the s*x and dating game:

1) **Don't take the person's word for it:** Here's a newsflash – people lie. A lot of men lie when it comes to getting the thing that they want the most and the smooth brother with all the swag got that way because he knows how to tell women exactly what they want to hear. Imagine being broke, hungry and trying to get into your favorite restaurant. That's how a man feels when he's trying to have s*x with you. Some guys will say anything to get what they want.

So, if you consider yourself responsible and ask a man about his HIV status, understand that pretty much every man is going to tell you that he's fine. Sometimes he's actually fine, sometimes he's not fine, and then much of the time, he may not be entirely sure that he's fine. However, he knows that if he gives you anything other than an entirely confident answer, you may second-guess your decision to sleep with him. Besides that, there are some men who really believe they're healthy when they're actually not. Why? Because a person who was tested for HIV two years ago and has had several partners since then doesn't really know if anything has changed in his status.

2) **Get tested together:** The best way to know if a person is safe is to see the test results for yourself and make sure they are recent. Don't take someone's word for it when your life is on the line. By not covering your bases, you're risking being sexually isolated for the rest of your life because of one toxic interaction. Don't put your fate in someone's word, especially when they might be tempted to stretch the truth to get something they really want from you.

3) **Get tested for EVERYTHING:** With all the talk about HIV testing, everyone seems to forget that there is a long

list of other STDs you can get besides HIV. Asking the doctor for a full STD panel is a good way to make sure that your partner isn't infected with anything. Even allowing him to give you oral s*x without proper protection is a great way for you to catch genital herpes. Don't assume that a person is entirely safe just because they are HIV-negative. If the person likes to "get around" sexually, there's a good chance that they have other diseases that have remained dormant in their body.

I hope these thoughts are helpful in your personal journey. s*x is a powerful drug that makes all of us do silly things. But at least speaking honestly about what's really going on is a good way to find our way to the truth. I wish you the best of luck.

Why Do Men Cheat? The New Movie That Landed in my Facebook

I received a preview for the new film, "Why Do Men Cheat" in my Facebook account today. I thought the title was interesting, since it asks one of those questions that nearly every woman in America has asked 10,000 girlfriends over the years. I enjoyed the preview, and I am always happy to support a project being done in the city of Detroit, one of the most creative and talented (yet troubled) places in America. The dating market in Detroit has become one where too many people have been taught to make war where there should be love, and male/female interactions are unlike anywhere else in the United States.

With that being said, I'd be remiss not to mention this new film without giving my top five thoughts on why men cheat. Again, I am not a relationship guru, but if Steve Harvey can give relationship advice then so can I. Here it goes:

1) **If you want to understand why men cheat, be prepared to hear the truth.** Accept the fact that men and women are biologically different, and there are certain things that men and women will never tell each other. Women usually lie about how many men they've been

with, and men lie about how many women they are thinking about right now. But if you open the door for truth, you can get it, just make sure you can handle what you see. Love is not a perfect fairytale, and the saddest thing in the world is to go through life searching for something that does not exist. The new guy might seem to be so much better than the last one, but that's usually because unlike his ex-girlfriends, you haven't had a chance to see his dirty laundry. This doesn't mean that all men cheat, but one can be easily deluded into thinking that the next person in line is the answer to all of our problems, when the last person we just left might have actually been pretty good.

2) **Human beings are mammals.** Mammals have mating patterns, whether they are deer in the woods or human beings in a corporate office. If you want to figure out what lies in the hearts of man, just watch the animals on the *Discovery Channel*. Bears do what they do without worrying about what society thinks, what their pastor is going to say or what is socially acceptable. They simply do what comes naturally. Most human beings do all the same stuff and have all the same impulses, we just convince ourselves that we're advanced enough to overcome our natural instincts. But whether you talk about animals or

people, the alpha male is always a mating target for females, males always seek females who show signs of fertility, females seek out strength and men have a tendency to sometimes roam. That's just the way it is (again, I am not justifying cheating or saying that it happens in all cases, so don't hang me for that one).

3) **Women who want to understand what men want and think should ask close male friends their thoughts, so they can get an honest assessment.** Your boyfriend does not have the proper incentives to tell you everything that he is thinking. The risk is too high and if he tells you everything, you are going to look at him with the side eye. Women say they want the truth, but the fact is that many of them actually prefer a well-positioned lie that is consistent with the fairytale of perfection that we want to believe our relationships possess. It's almost like how people might criticize a movie by saying that "it's not realistic," when we know that movies are never realistic, that's why they're called movies. What we are really saying in that case is that we'd like to see an unrealistic portrayal of highly realistic events that fits the mold of a fantasy that we find to be emotionally stimulating. That's why, in many cases, you may be actually asking men to tell either tell

you a comfortable truth or an equally comfortable lie to give you emotional stimulation and security.

If you really want to know what's going on with me, an intelligent male friend or a brother can give you the information you need. You can also learn a lot from a book. I learned a great deal about women by reading the book, "What Women Want Men to Know," by psychologist Barbara D'Angelis. What I read both traumatized and enlightened me, for I learned that men and women really are from different planets. As you go down the rabbit hole of understanding, be prepared to accept the truth and stop thinking that life is a perfect little fantasy.

4) **Younger men are more prone to cheating than older men, mainly because higher testosterone levels lead to s*x drives that are through the roof.** Unfortunately, for some men (say, an alpha male like Kobe Bryant), even the most beautiful woman in the world (i.e. his wife Vanessa) may not be enough to keep him entirely focused (hence the whole nasty situation with the girl in Colorado back in 2004 after everyone warned Kobe not to get married so young). What's really odd is that even though he's cheated on Vanessa incessantly, Kobe believes in his heart that he loves her. That's largely because for

many men, their hearts and their s*x organs work in different departments and have very little to do with one another. He shows his love for Vanessa by paying her bills, taking her with him in public and raising kids with her. These are the sacrifices that men make when they love a woman; his p***s manages about 2% of his life.

5) **Accept the fact that you can't control everything in your relationship.** Going through someone's phone, email account or text messages only makes you nuts. If you think your partner is cheating and you can't handle it, then just leave. What I did learn a long time, ago, however, is that you gain very little comfort by spying on every aspect of another person's life. The truth is that there are always going to be things that they do and think that you'll never know anything about. The best assessment you can make is whether or not your instincts tell you that the person loves you and makes you their top priority. If someone loves you, you've got something valuable. How you deal with the cheating is up to you, but the reality is that most couples that have been together in those 50 year marriages you might fantasize about have typically overcome some form of infidelity.....just go talk to one of them and they can tell you their war stories.

Once again, life is not a fairytale. Lasting relationships can be ugly and difficult work. If you're not ready to do the work, then stop hoping for the fantasy and stop presuming that the next guy on the list is so much better than the rest. Finding good love and keeping it is hard work and happens from the heart up, not the waste down. At least that's my perception.

The Worst Celebrity Parents Ever, The Dream and Christina – What We Can Learn

The nasty divorce between The Dream and Christina Milian is about as ugly as a relationship can get. Christina goes onto the radio to say that her child's father is absent and openly auditions for a new father to her child. That leads to The Dream going onto Twitter and bashing his child's mother as a "has-been" and a gold digger.

When you look at situations like this one, you are reminded of just how ugly some of our relationships can get when we have two massive egos colliding like Supernovas in the Milk Way. All the while, the person who suffers the most is the poor child who has the misfortune of being caught in the crossfire of two adults with relentless egos. It's just sad.

Not that I am big on celebrity relationships, but I watch them because other people are watching them. I then think about what these relationships say about our own situations and how we can do a better job of raising our kids. The dating scene is like a big thunderstorm and although you have to leave the house, you might want to make sure you're wearing an umbrella. This kind of messy drama can catch any of us.

Five Questions Men Should Ask Themselves Before Having s*x

I've been a black man for quite a while now. It's been a fun ride, with its ups and downs. But I have to say that in this journey, where half the world is working to secure your extinction, you realize that your ability to think and make critical decisions can become the key to your survival. But beyond surviving, you also want to prosper. Part of your path to prosperity should include good family planning.

Kids are expensive, both financially and emotionally. When they come to life, your life suddenly becomes secondary. You might want the new Xbox360 game, but you won't be playing jack if the baby needs a new set of diapers. Even if you try to walk away from your responsibility, the courts won't let you, and you'll also be explaining to a 20-year old boy why you hated him enough to leave him to the wolves.

Given that s*x is one of the most natural forces in the universe, I thought I'd explain a few things to you. You don't have to take my advice, and I don't know everything. But when it's all said and done and you are lying in the bed you've made for yourself, you'll realize that the most significant events in your life come down to whether or not you made good choices or bad ones. Here are five things to consider before having s*x:

1) Why are you doing this anyway?

Sadly enough, commercialized hip hop on the radio makes its billions by teaching black men to have s*x with any pretty thing with a working female organs. The rule is that if she's "fine" and she's willing, then you'd be a fool not to take it. The sad part of this story is that a lot of brothers soon find that a toxic woman, even one with a beautiful smile, can make you wish you were never born. Evelyn Lozada, the violent Sasquatch on *Basketball Wives*, might be a perfect case-in-point. In addition to women who can be flat out evil and devious, there are others who are walking public health alerts. Everything that looks clean is not. Speaking of which...

2) Diseases are everywhere

When's the last time you went to the doctor to get tested for STDs? Not just HIV, but Gonorrhea, Chlamydia, Syphilis, Herpes, HPV and all the other things that can kill you? Are you really stupid enough to think that you can run through every woman you want and not catch at least two or three of these diseases (yes, even with a condom, since a lot of people don't wear condoms when they have oral s*x)? Everyone wants to blame gay black men for the fact that HIV rates among black women are through the roof, but an irresponsible heterosexual is far more devastating than a responsible gay man any day of the week.

3) Are you ready for kids?

Newsflash: There tends to be a correlation between s****l activity and child birth. Babies are not delivered by Storks, they are delivered by baby's mamas. Some people talk about "hitting that" and "getting it in," as if there is no chance that this woman might eventually be running around with the your child in her womb. When you choose to sleep with a woman, you may be putting your life and your child's life in that woman's hands. This leads to our next question...

4) Would you want this woman to be the mother of your child?

Sooo, you're about to plant your seed of life into the woman that you don't know, don't like and don't want to hang around more than 10 minutes after the s*x is over? Good choice. How about spending the next 30 years with this woman, as she conspires to keep you out of the life your child, sucks up a massive chunk of your paycheck and teaches your kids all the wrong values, with you being able to do nothing about it? Your seed is valuable, and you shouldn't share it with just any woman who opens herself up to you. You have to think about your future.

Speaking of child support...

5) Do you want to pay child support for the rest of your life? Let me answer that question—no you don't. Terrell Owens once thought it was a GOOD thing that he had as many women as he wanted. Now, he's slowly realizing that his blessing has turned into a curse. The man who once had money to the ceiling is now taking a bath in his own pity party. Terrell didn't plan, and all the other dudes out there making babies like there's no tomorrow will also expect someone to feel sorry for them years later when they are broke, busted and disgusted. The truth is that I don't feel sorry for them, and if you make the same choices, the world won't feel sorry for you either.

S*x is thrilling, amazing and incredibly powerful. In fact, the drive for s*x can make a man insane. But as Spiderman's uncle once said (I really love this quote and I use it all the time) "with great power comes great responsibility," and with manhood comes accountability. Little boys have no business having s*x with anyone, so when you share yourself with a woman in the future, you must make sure that you're thinking like a man.

Single Moms, Be Careful About The Men You Allow Around Your Kids

When I was a youth track coach a decade ago, I found that running with the kids every day was like a fountain of youth. The experience transformed me for life and was one of the most rewarding things I've ever done. The parents loved me, and I loved (most of) them. But I must confess years later that I look back and find myself shocked at how so many of these parents (especially single Moms) trusted a grown man around their children.

Jerry Sandusky, the former football coach at Penn State, also made himself out to be a role model for "lost" children. He, too, said he loved his kids and took pleasure in spending time with them. He even formed a charity around the idea and was hailed by the community as a savior for lost kids who didn't have much parental support. The problem is that Sandusky loved his young, male football players for reasons that are both repulsive and unforgivable.

He and other sexual predators often present their affection toward children as a carefully veiled disguise for their desire to take advantage of youth who don't have adults to protect them.

These "lost children" — who don't have a father in the home — become targets of child predators in the same way pimps prey on young girls with low self-esteem.

One of the saddest effects of the breakdown of the Black family is that many of our kids experience sexual abuse because someone is allowed in their lives who doesn't belong. Single mothers, who are desperate to find male role models for their children, can sometimes leave their kids vulnerable to any man who takes an interest without wondering if they may be putting their child in harm's way. A mother looking for love may allow a strange man around her kids, not knowing that this man is lustfully observing her teenage daughter or son.

This happens more often than you might think. Oftentimes, we don't find out about the abuse until years later, after the damage is done. In many cases, we don't find out about it at all. The truth is that we must teach our kids to identify sexual abuse when they see it and to alert an adult when it happens.

Many black moms worry incessantly about whether or not their man is secretly gay (thanks to Oprah Winfrey and the "down low" effect). But I don't hear nearly as much chatter about whether or not your man is the kind of guy that will sleep with a 15-year old. Many millions of Americans will shake their butts in a minute to an R. Kelly song, but care nothing about the fact that there is a substantial amount of evidence (and a videotape) suggesting that he has an interest in women as young as 12 years old. Sexual abuse is real in our community and we must confront it.

We have to warn our kids on how to identify sexual abuse when they see it, and how to report it to adults. Once we receive this information, we must act on it without hesitation. Also, remember that human sexuality is a deep abyss for some, containing secrets that they guard to the death. So just because a man is nice to your kids, that doesn't mean that he's right for them. You must vet people carefully when they come around those you love.

What I Learned from the Greatest Marriage Proposal Ever

The recent viral video of a random white dude proposing to his girlfriend sent chills down my spine. I am not a hopeless romantic, but I am hopelessly in love with the potential and future of the black family in America. For some reason, there was something about this video that lit a fuse in its viewers, leading me to reflect on some of the barriers that keep all of us from showing our best selves when we enter into relationships.

I am no relationship guru, but I resubmit that if Steve Harvey is qualified to talk about relationships, then so am I. When I speak with my daughters about love, I think about the bitterness that some of us can have from past disappointments, creating a tough shell of cold disregard to protect the most vulnerable part of our spirit. We enter relationships with itchy trigger fingers and toxic predispositions, causing us to wait for the other person to do something that will confirm that he/she is the dog that we expect that person to be.

In the black community, the lack of trust between men and women can sometimes turn love into war. Starting with the first disappointments from the missing father or a college heartbreak, love can become an exercise of saving face and not being played, which is not conducive to building lasting families. As a result, divorce rates are through the roof, babymama-itis is at an all-time high, and STD rates are skyrocketing as people in their twenties and thirties bounce from one broken relationship to another.

What I enjoyed about this video is that there is something amazing that happens when one party doesn't allow fear to keep him/her from expressing deep-seated affection for another person. The man in this video made himself look like a d**n fool to show this woman how much he loves her. Not to say that we should get all of our cues from white people (you know how I feel about that, they are no better than us), but there is something that can be learned from everyone, and this guy teaches all of us a great lesson on love.

If your relationships consistently fall apart, or you find that your so-called love life has become a haven of treachery and emotional espionage, you might want to take a look in the mirror and determine if the person you see is emotionally equipped to take the risks necessary to experience true love. You must also determine if you are capable of identifying people who will reflect that love back at you and not selfishly absorb it in order to maintain control. Without taking risk, there is little reward, so you can't expect to witness the highs of lasting love if you live life with your cards held close to your vest.

That's what I learned from the random white dude proposing to his girlfriend.

When Michelle Almost Left Barack – What This Tells Us About Love and Life

A new book says that in the year 2000, Michelle Obama prepared divorce papers that were going to be used to part ways with her husband, Barack. The new book, "The Amateur" by former *New York Times Magazine* Editor Edward Klein, also claims that some of Barack's friends felt that he might even be suicidal as a result of the split. "After Obama's humiliating defeat, he was broke and deeply in debt and it looked as though he might be finished in public life," wrote Klein.

> "During the dark days that followed his defeat, he turned to Michelle for comfort. But she was in no mood to offer him sympathy. After all he had refused to listen to her warnings about taking on the formidable Bobby Rush. He had put his family in a precarious financial position. And he had dashed Michelle's hopes of creating a stable and secure future."

I am not sure what Klein's objectives are in writing this book, for he is obviously biased. The use of selective information, as well as his imbalanced analysis of the Israeli-Palestinian conflict, shows that he clearly has an agenda. But that's not the issue, at least as far as I'm concerned.

What I find most interesting about the book is that Klein's "explosive" revelations about the Obamas are built upon tearing down the "perfect loving couple" image that the Obamas have worked so hard to cultivate. He tells us that the Obama marriage isn't as perfect as it may seem, which might throw some people off.

I am, however, quite happy that some of this "damning" information about the Obama marriage has been made public, in the same way I had no problem with historians revealing that Dr. Martin Luther King might have had extramarital affairs. It is sometimes necessary to be soaked in a bath of ice cold realism to get us to let go of crippling illusions of endless marital bliss.

The Obama family has been seen as a model relationship for millions of African Americans across the country. Scores of women want to be like Michelle and some are seeking their own Barack. But the truth is that we can sometimes seek to fulfill our ambitions without a realistic assessment of the challenges that might lie before us.

While many black women might want to be like Michelle, the fact is that most women don't have what it takes.

Most long-term marriages are not the cute fairy tales of continuous excitement that some people might expect. Instead, succeeding at marriage can be like winning a long and b****y war, where your friends have died along the way, and you've endured nightmares that lie beyond your wildest dreams. The sacrifices can be immeasurable and those who survive are able to make it through with sheer determination and singularity of purpose. The words "I will not quit" can be critical in getting your b**t to the finish line.

Black women who are looking for their own Barack Obama might need to take a hint from the good and bad decisions of Michelle. On one hand, the fact that she was able to ride with Barack through the bad times to get to the good means that she deserves credit for her determination. After all, they did go broke as he pursued his "unrealistic" goal of one day becoming the first black president.

At the same time, a lesson can be learned by the mistake that Michelle almost made: Giving up on her man during his darkest moments. While one cannot be certain of the circumstances that led Michelle to consider leaving Barack, the fact is that a good woman does all she can to support her man even during the toughest of times. If Michelle wasn't ready for the difficult and volatile ride she might endure to get to the top, then she could have easily married someone with more stable and "realistic" ambitions. One of the greatest fears of any man who might consider marriage is that his spouse will only support his dream when it is profitable to do so.

So far, the Klein book is proving one simple fact: The Obama marriage isn't perfect. But if you didn't know that from the beginning, then you really haven't lived. Marriage is not a fairy tale, even if you are in the Oval Office. It's one of the most difficult things you'll ever do.

A Quick Thought on Why You Can't "Find a Good Man/Woman"

When I hear people say, "I can't find a good man/woman," that statement makes me think. I believe it is more of a reflection of you being less interested in being with someone who is good for your long-term well-being than being with the person who gives you instant gratification (even horribly bad mates can make us feel oh so good).

Therefore, the difference is no more confusing than the way overweight people pass up healthy food so they can find the greasy, sweet dishes that tingle their taste buds. When that person says, "I can't find healthy food," they are actually saying "I can't find any healthy food that tastes as good as this cheeseburger, so I am going to just keep eating at McDonald's." Until the person makes a conscious decision to make the sacrifices necessary to eat healthy food, they are always going to experience the ups and downs that come with a lifetime of grease and fat.

My thinking on the issue? Understanding yourself and finding a way to navigate the fickle and powerful balance between what you want and what you need can take you a long way. So, whether you are a 300 pound man seeking to get the body of an athlete, a comedian trying to get your first big break or a saddened soul with a consistently broken heart, most of us know when unhealthy choices have served to poison our lives and our bodies.

When we make bad choices and the consequences come home to roost, we cannot look at the world as the cause of our personal failures. There is also a tremendous amount of accountability that must come from within. Blaming the world for your disappointment is like traveling down a road with no end. But when you do get to the end of that road, you find that it started and ended inside of YOU.

We Often Discuss Deadbeat Dads, but What about Deadbeat Mothers?

Most of us know the narrative of the deadbeat dad: The man who shows up to make babies, but never comes by to take care of them. Maybe he doesn't pay child support, doesn't spend time with his children, or has more babies mamas than the local maternity ward. I get it, we've heard it. We know that horrible fathers exist, and that they should be confronted like the terrorists that they are to the black community.

But the untold story is that of the deadbeat mother. She often slips under the radar because the "N*ggers ain't s**t" rhetoric drowns out the voices of her defenseless children who are suffering under her regime of blatant selfishness and irresponsibility. Like former North Korean Dictator Kim Jong II, the deadbeat mom reigns supreme over the lives of her kids, seeing them as possessions rather than real human beings. The words "my babies" come out of her mouth like a pimp claiming hookers on the corner, or a farmer talking about a flock of pigs that he keeps in his barn. Her children have become a weapon.

When it comes to the deadbeat mom, the non-existent father never had a chance, as she straps on male genitalia and demands that people send her a Father's Day card every year. In fact, the father might have been dismissed before the baby shower. Yes, she's doing it all by herself, but doesn't know the difference between raising kids and teaching them to be successful, productive and well-balanced human beings. Since her kids don't complain about the psychological damage being done during the parenting process, she presumes that everything must be OK.

When I participated in the Fatherhood tour with former NBA player Etan Thomas, I heard stories about fathers who might have been victims of the deadbeat mom. These were men who desperately wanted to see their children, but were blocked at every turn by a Maternal Security Force that had become convinced that she'd created the babies all by herself.

One man told me that he'd been required to pay child support for years, but that the courts wouldn't even tell him where they were sending the money so he could track down the mother of his child in order to see his son. It appeared that his son's mother had decided that she wanted access to his money, but was unwilling to share any of the parental power. This reminds me of how the

Democrats convince black people to vote for them so they can ignore black issues and spend their time fighting for gay rights and immigration.

Another person reached out to tell me about a teen girl who'd been sexually a*******d by one of her mother's boyfriends. As the endless parade of random men were being brought into the household and being asked to babysit, the child's mother was oblivious to the idea that thousands of children are abused every year by their mother's boyfriends. When the child mentioned the abuse to her mother, the little girl was punished for lying, and the mother continued to live her life as if everything were just fine. Few stories have ever made me want to use a gun as much as this one.

One of the greatest myths in the on-going conversation about the breakdown of the black family is that every woman with a functioning womb is equipped to be a good mom. That's just flat out wrong, I don't care how many ABC News specials try to blame everything on black men. The fact that your kids are in your home does not make you a good steward of their future.

Not acknowledging the need for strong male role models (preferably the dad) can lead you to raising your boys to remain little boys into adulthood, thus ruining another woman's husband. You think you did a great job with your son, but notice that 20 years later, he's a pants-sagging, uneducated, wannabe thug who sits in his mama's basement playing Xbox all day in order to avoid paying child support. Even worse is that the deadbeat mom loves having her 30-year old son in the house because he has taken over the role of her missing husband.

Most of us know that bad parenting exists across both genders. We also know that bad parenting can be predicated on making really bad choices. The best way for men to overcome a deadbeat mother is to avoid choosing one. The idea that you should place your p*enis into any functioning v@gina attached to a pretty face is one of the easiest ways to end up stressed out because your child is being raised by a stripper.

Family planning should start with simply having a plan. That plan begins with being thoughtful about where you choose to place your seed. Yes, I know that rappers on the radio tell men that they should sleep with every girl who offers to give them what they want, but what rappers don't tell you is that this is where unwanted babies come from. In fact, the easiest way for a man to spend his life financially devastated is to have a bunch of children out of wedlock. The courts will eat your bank account alive and not feel the least bit sorry for you, just ask fallen NFL star Terrell Owens.

When it comes to mothers, old and young, it's always important to understand that you didn't create the baby by yourself. You have a co-parent, and he has the same rights that you do. You may not like his girlfriend, where he lives, what he does for a living or how he disciplines your child, but he is your child's father. You chose to sleep with him, and thus made a lifetime pact to share parental rights and responsibilities, even if he is not the father you'd like for him to be. Of course there are exceptions, but it seems that we live in an era where people are more likely to discard inconvenient relationships instead of working to improve them.

When I speak to my daughters about men, I tell them that "If a man doesn't appear to be someone who'd make a good husband or father, don't even give him your phone number. If you can't tell if he'd be a good father, that means you don't know him well enough to be sleeping with him, and you should probably keep your distance." Your children should not be the product of a one night stand where you were seduced out of your clothes by "bad boy swag." Our kids deserve better than that, and a tragic life is easily built on a pile of spontaneous mistakes.

Also, parents should realize that being ADDICTED to your child is not the same as LOVING your child. The "Motherholic addiction" is when you can't live without your child, need your child nearby and snuggle with your child so your brain can be hit with constant fixes of the neurotransmitter Oxytocin (aka "the love drug") necessary to keep you from feeling lonely in your life. Truly loving your child means making difficult sacrifices so your offspring can have a productive and positive future. It might mean putting up with a dad who differs from you in parenting style, or knowing the difference between being a parent to your child and being a buddy.

To men who find themselves locking horns with a deadbeat mom, I recommend securing your rights in the womb. That means going to court early to set up visitation, and fighting for space in the life of your kids. I also recommend being thoughtful about the women you share your body with. Your child is usually better off if you keep your family together in the first place—I don't care what anyone else says, children are typically happier with two parents than they are with just one. I speak from personal experience after having a child at the age of 18 and paying a huge price for the next 25 years. We all make mistakes and I've surely made a share of my own.

It's time to modify the story when it comes to the state of the black family in America. The whole idea that black men are ignorant, lazy cavemen who throw their offspring out with the trash is tired, inaccurate and ultimately disrespectful. This certainly doesn't let men off the hook for the role we play in our personal and collective outcomes. But it does mean that we have to broaden the conversation.

Soooo, Black Women Can't Find Good Men? Oh Really?

I watched an *ABC News* special the other night featuring Steve Harvey, Jacque Reed, Sherri Shepherd and my homeboys Hill Harper and Jimi Izrael. The show covered a tried and true topic that is sure to get sky high ratings from the black community: The topic was: Why successful black women can't find a good man. I am not going to risk bringing on the wrath of black women by saying things that some of them may not want to hear, but I have to be honest about what I saw on this show. Let me just cut to the chase and lay the issues out one-by-one:

1) **Why are black women taking relationship advice from Steve Harvey?** Not to disrespect Steve's ability to drop knowledge, but isn't he a comedian? If we are taking relationship advice from a comedian and our relationship turns into a joke, who do we blame in the end? Bottom line—perhaps learning how to love another person means that after you put aside the book by the comedian, you should go out and buy a book by a relationship expert.

2) **Most good women have little trouble getting married to decent men:** One has to be skeptical of the beautiful, intelligent, fully capable woman who simply says

that she can't find a good man anywhere. Most women I know who are well-balanced and who also appreciate the idea of respecting men in the same way they would like to be respected, have no trouble finding suitable mates. Sorry to break this to you, but the only constant variable in your relationships is a person called YOU. Rather than pointing the finger at the world, a bit more introspection might be called for: perhaps you have to reconsider your laundry list of expectations or wonder if you're not doing a good job finding men who are open to commitment. It's easy to find a man, just not easy to find a man who is willing to be with you and you only; a lot of brothers simply play the field and allow you to buy an emotional lottery ticket, hoping that you'll be the one he selects in the end. You may be fishing in the wrong ponds in the first place or using the wrong bait to catch the fish you're bringing home.

3) **If you want something bad enough, take a class:** There are classes on relationships and marriage out there that don't cost much money. If you are determined to be the best mate you can possibly be, it might make sense to take a class that explains all the subtleties and challenges of making a relationship work (not just the counseling you get from your pastor). A relationship is not about a mate

fulfilling your long and detailed list of needs and expectations. The bottom line is that if you hope to receive more, you must first fully commit yourself to giving more. Some of us are taught that we should expect the world and not offer anything in return: that's a perfect recipe for getting dumped.

4) **Big mistake – always chasing the alpha male:** I know a lot of "regular guys" who are unable to find a woman that is interested in being with them. This is especially true in their mid-twenties, when everyone is single and living fancy-free, with little expectation for long-term commitment. Some of the women these "regular guys" are interested in are not paying them much attention to them, mainly because the woman has become enchanted with the dream-like alpha male in her life: the guy who fits every single portion of the checklist (height, income, education, toe nail length, swag, etc.), but who may not be available for a monogamous, long-term relationship. What many women seem to forget is that there are some men who always have room for another woman on the roster. If you're wasting all your time with the lying, cheating, super dog, you might miss out on the chance to be with the man who will love you forever and father all of your children. He may not come in the same

package, and by comparing the two without considering the differences in what each of them offers, you may be passing up on your opportunity.

5) **Relationships should not be a pissing contest:** One of the by-products of many black children growing up in single parent homes is that their relationships become highly contentious. I once saw a neck swinging, energized woman say, "I need a man who can handle me!" What I wanted to tell her is that your man should not have to "handle" you as if you are a wild bull with his testicles sewn together. The act of love is a process of being open, feeling and sharing, not trying to dominate one another. So, if you need to be "handled" in your relationships, realize that you are likely going to only attract men who are mean, rough and insensitive enough to handle you effectively. In fact, you're not searching for a mate, you may be actually looking for a pimp. Fighting and domination is not the same as love – let's not get it twisted.

6) **There's nothing wrong with a few gender roles:** Sherri Shepherd, during an especially volatile segment of the ABC News show, swung her hands around in the air saying, "I don't have time to validate you every day!" –

referring to the fact that she doesn't feel that it's her job to make her man feel good about himself on a regular basis. What's interesting is that most women want their man to make them feel beautiful and to feel like a woman. So, why is it not acceptable for a man to expect his wife to make him feel like a man? A man doesn't want to marry another guy—or a woman who feels that any and all gender roles are an insult to her feminine independence and then also expect that same man to be willing to be regularly emasculated. It's O.K. to make your man feel like he's THE man, a king and a leader. A good man will surely return the favor and make you feel like a beautiful woman.

7) **Let's be real—many men aren't as excited about marriage as women:** As much as we want to believe that men grow up fantasizing about their wedding day the same way that many women do, the truth is that this is not the case. Many men see marriage as a frightening commitment that will cause them to be vilified for actions they can engage in without consequence when they are single (notice the millions of dollars that Shaquille O'Neal and the rapper Nas have paid to get out of their marriages – every man gets petrified when he reads these stories).

A woman who gets her husband is the one who makes the man WANT to be married: she makes him feel free, strong, needed, loved and supported. While this may seem to be a primitive concept, the reality is that the reverse is true for sex: Men and women both want it, but men know they have to work just a little bit harder to "get some." They've got to buy flowers, take the woman to dinner, and make her feel comfortable. It would be silly for a man to think that a woman should buy him flowers and beg him to have sex with her. The converse is true for marriage—where getting a man to overcome his anxiety is a great way to get him to give you what you want.

I love black women: My mother, daughter and grandmother are black women and there is not a more precious group of women on the planet. But the truth is that this "woe is me, black men ain't sh*t" attitude has to be replaced with something more constructive. If not, we'll be having these same forums 20 years from today.

Chapter 7

We are the Answers that We Seek

Black Media is dead; Maybe It's Time for a Resurrection

My favorite show in the world is "Open Line," which is co-hosted by Bob Slade, James Mtume and Bob Pickett. In fact, as a man who turns down 99% of all interview requests I receive, this is the only show I appear on, basically any time they need my help. I hate nearly all interviews because I'm so busy, but this is one that makes me happy.

"Open Line" is one of the only issue-oriented talk shows on black radio in the country, and certainly the only one I know of that draws such a massive audience. Every time I appear on the show, I get text messages and emails from scores of New Yorkers who gained something from the dialogue on the show. It's not to say that other shows couldn't do the same if they were given the opportunity, but black media has changed for the worse over the last 20 years.

Not only has black media changed, some would say that it is effectively dead. It's been reduced, for the most part, to a few corporate owned online outlets, many of whom are more loyal to the Democratic Party than the black community. There are also a couple of popular national radio shows that are convinced that it's more important to make black people laugh than it is to challenge them to think. I won't talk about television, unless you want to discuss the way Viacom-owned BET has single-handedly lowered the collective IQ of the entire black community by no less than 35 points.

Black journalists are in a similar predicament, where asking critical questions on black politics means that Valerie Jarrett is going to ban you from the White House. They may also find themselves struggling with low-paying jobs with media outlets that don't allow them to pursue meaningful work that is all that reflective of their authentic selves. When a young woman asked me about starting a career in journalism, I really didn't know what to say.

"Open Line" is now working to become "Open Line Nation," hosted on Sirius/XM, and I hope they achieve their objective. The loss of black media has made it difficult for black people to communicate with one another en masse and have the conversations that need to be had about our issues. These are not discussions that need to be sanctioned by the ever watchful overseers in the Obama Administration. They should not be pre-approved by corporate America. There must be a family dialogue, where all views, conservative and liberal, are brought to the table, and our community's prosperity and survival are more important than anything else.

I hope you'll join me in supporting this outstanding show. I also hope you'll support our push to get the Federal Communications Commission to break up monopolies within media that have turned nearly every black radio station in the country into a mindless drone for Clear Channel. Our kids don't need to be raised with an unhealthy dose of toxic hip-hop on the way back to school each morning. We also don't need watered-down "Black leadership brought to you by Wal-mart." Instead, we need something that is strong, thoughtful and conscientious to help us become our best selves.

It's time to talk about our media.

Muhammad Ali Shows Up at the Olympics: Why He's the Greatest Athlete of All-Time

It was over 50 years ago that the great Muhammad Ali held up his own gold medal at the 1960 Olympics. Ali would later go on to become the youngest heavyweight champion in history. Ali showed up again at this year's Olympic Games, in his old form, with the same old swag that made him the legend that he is today. While he certainly can't move and talk like he did as a young man, the world knows that on the inside, he's still one of the most engaging figures in the world.

Ali wore a white suit during the ceremony and looked like a man who is tired and frail. But his presence is powerful. He was diagnosed with Parkinson's disease 30 years ago after being hit in the head so many times during his boxing career. His journey is a warning to young fighters about staying in the sport too long.

Ali's wife Lonnie was his savior. A woman who'd admired him since she was a little girl stepped in when his last ex-wife abandoned him and took over his business empire. She turned Ali from a tired, broke old athlete into the icon that he is today. Lonnie's work shows us that a great woman can make a man far better off than he was before. She has truly been his guardian angel.

With Ali being from my hometown of Louisville, my relationship with him has been one that has lasted a lifetime. I remember hearing stories from friends and relatives about Ali's life as a young man, and I have his picture in my living room, next to my other adopted father, Malcolm X. As a graduate student, I used to read stories about Ali's life to give me inspiration to overcome the adversity in my own life. My simple philosophy was, "If he can overcome all of that, then I can fight through the racism in my own world. These people can't hold me back if I stick to what I believe in." So, I was one of those little boys who Ali inspired to realize his own potential and I thank God that he didn't just live life for himself.

The Olympic appearance by Ali was to raise money for the Muhammad Ali Center in Louisville, KY. There is also Generation Ali, a social media site to educate young people about the values that Ali embraced. This is the second major appearance by Ali, after his presence at the games in 1996 brought the crowd to their feet in tears. That was 16 years ago, and at that time, he was able to actually walk up the steps and light the torch himself.

Most ironic about Ali's appearance at the Olympics this year is that he was not quite welcome at the Olympics during the 1960s. In 1968, during the black power protest by John Carlos and Tommy Smith, one of their demands was that Ali be reinstated as world boxing champ. Ali's title had been taken by the authorities, who wanted him to fight in the Vietnam War.

"When Ali put everything he achieved on the line in difference to his religion and political principles that got attention around the world," said Sociologist Dr. Harry Edwards. "People eventually came to believe Ali was sincere and over time there developed a tremendous degree of unquestioned integrity about him."

Ali shows all of us that if you stick with what you believe in and never give up, there is always a brighter day around corner. He is also a clear reminder that a great athlete is more than just a man who can run and jump on the field. Instead, he is a man who is willing to fight for something greater than himself.

That's why, to this day, Muhammad Ali was a runaway favorite ahead of Michael Jordan in the *Sports Illustrated* vote for the greatest athlete of the last 100 years. He didn't dominate Jordan because of his skill. Instead, Ali dominated Jordan because he was a greater man than Michael Jordan ever wanted to be. He knew that his real power was not in his arms and legs, but understood the awesome ability of a great athlete to elevate his people and change the world. That's what true greatness is all about.

Chicago Officials Welcome the Support of Louis Farrakhan to Stop Inner City Violence

The city of Chicago is welcoming the help of Min. Louis Farrakhan in the fight to clear the streets of Chicago of its spike in violence.

"Whatever we can do to help stop violence, I'm for it — no matter who it comes from. Just like CeaseFire. They have ex-offenders helping to stop the violence. It doesn't matter, as long as we can stop people from getting killed," Ald. Walter Burnett told the *Chicago Sun-Times*.

"I don't agree with some of [Farrakhan's] statements. I don't agree with everything everybody does. But, I do agree with people who are trying to help us save lives." Ald. Leslie Hairston says that she is "in regular conversation" with Farrakhan and the Nation of Islam to find ways to curb the violence in the city.

"They are extremely well-organized. They are known for their discipline. That brings attention to the community," Hairston said.

"Any group that is willing to do something to help fight the violence — they're welcome."

Farrakhan and the Nation of Islam have stepped up to the plate to help stop the violence in Chicago. The city has been decimated with a huge spike in violent crimes and homicides, with most of these homicides being black-on-black.

The men, known as the Fruit of Islam, presented themselves last month after 7-year old Heaven Sutton was killed by stray bullets. Heaven is not the only child to have died in recent months. Children of all ages are in such danger that they are unable to even walk to school in some neighborhoods.
CeaseFire, an organization designed to stop the violence, is partnering with the city to mediate gang disputes and help to stop shootings. But the Chicago Fraternal Order of Police is against the alliance, largely due to the fact that the organization is refusing to share its information with police.

But Pat Camden, a spokesperson for the FOP, says that Farrakhan's participation is more than welcome.

"The last time I checked, Fruit of Islam isn't convicted felons, are they? That's a huge difference. And they're not getting paid by the city," Camden said.

"Anything that will cut down on the violence because of the lack of manpower, we're glad to see. It's people in the community getting involved to stop the violence. He's part of the community."

Even Mayor Rahm Emanuel said that Farrakhan's support is fine and welcome. "Everyone has a role to play in reducing violence. We all must do our part to make sure our communities are safe," said Emanuel's communications director Sarah Hamilton.

The city of Chicago is desperate because they are faced with a problem that its political leaders cannot solve. The violence that the city has long ignored is starting to stain their national reputation, reducing the numbers of businesses and tourists who feel safe coming to the city. No one wants to visit an Americanized version of Beirut, and Chicago is beginning to be known as a perfect place to die.

There is no reason that anyone should object to Farrakhan's support in stopping the violence. He has a unique ability to go places that no one else can go and persuade people who some consider to be unreachable. The Nation of Islam has the ability to command respect and produce discipline in even the most challenged black men, a valuable skill that should be harnessed and supported in every way imaginable.

The city shouldn't just provide verbal support to Min. Farrakhan's initiative, they should provide significant financial support. The South Side of Chicago deserves millions in reparations from the city for years of neglect, leading to inadequate schools, few job opportunities, police brutality/false incarceration and few activities for youth to distract them from participating in gang activity. Some of this money should be put into the hands of those with the bravery to go into the streets and protect little girls like Heaven Sutton.

The future of Chicago might depend heavily on the city's decision to support Minister Farrakhan. He's 80-years old, so they cannot allow this opportunity to pass them by. Farrakhan is a great American for making this sacrifice, and this fact should not be ignored.

What Happens to "Us" When Obama Is No Longer President?

Black history may soon find that it is defined by one line of demarcation: BB (Before Obama) and AB (After Obama). There might even be some historical reference to the volatile period called DB (During Obama), where an archive will contain images of black people going to blows over where our community should be positioned on the Obama issue.

The Obama presidency, unfortunately, has done more to divide black leadership than any event in the last 100 years. There are those who've chosen to side with the winning team, refusing to critique the Obama Administration on even the tiniest issues. Such criticism is readily interpreted as an assault on the absolute dictatorial authority that the Obama Administration seeks to maintain over African American political activity; they give us their agenda, not the other way around. The seemingly silly idea of "free Democratic thought" is as dead as the 8-track tape.

Then, there are those who challenge Obama to varying degrees. Some provide reasonable and justifiable concerns, while there are some who criticize the president without trying to even observe the pragmatic limitations of running the most powerful (and racist) nation on earth. One can't help but notice how factions of black leadership have formed as a result of the Obama presidency, with pro-Obama leaders on one side, and "Not-so-pro Obama" leaders on the other. Mind you, they all voted for Obama; but it's the depth of your love and loyalty for the administration that determines if you are considered to be a "hater" or not. For the record, asking the wrong questions or requesting any degree of accountability whatsoever defines you to be a hater.

One of the questions that attorney Karen Wallace posed to me the other day was: "What happens after Barack Obama is no longer President of the United States?" Sadly enough for those who love Barack Obama like a husband, best friend, boyfriend or baby daddy, the truth is that he can only be in the White House for another four years. As President Obama retires to Martha's Vineyard with the other Harvard alums, many of the most honest advocates for black America may no longer be empowered to fight for our causes. I doubt that President Obama will be volunteering to take their place.

To some extent, the black community is going through a period that can be compared to high school, where the issues we face over a four year period seem as if they will matter for the rest of our lives. Once high school was over, some realized that attempting suicide over a broken relationship or telling your parents that you hate them might have been an immature way to deal with a transitory situation.

In correlation, undermining the credibility of black public figures who've served the community for decades (e.g. Jeremiah Wright) might not be the best way to defend a man who will be out of office by the year 2016. We must learn how to love President Obama while simultaneously supporting advocates for our community, and honestly realize that one is not a substitute for the other. It is possible to take advantage of the present without mortgaging the future. Integration into the White House is not the same as building an independently prosperous community that doesn't need white American validation in order to be strong.

My point is not to say that the Obama presidency should not be respected or supported. Instead, it is to say that the divides in black leadership that have been caused by the Obama presidency must heal quickly in order for us to move forward as a collective. Also, no group of politicians should be allowed to play black public figures against one another by rewarding some for their loyalty and blocking others from having access to the negotiating table. Divide and conquer is a common political tactic, and it ultimately leads us to waste our votes by providing political support without having a clear agenda. The bottom line is that Obama is not going to be president forever, and we've got to have a Plan B.

Thank You Eric Holder, You Brought Me to Tears

Today, my brain froze in its tracks. I found myself speechless, yet full of enough energy to power a nuclear warhead. The emotions bounced around my insides like disco lights, and I found myself more sensitive to my environment than I'd been since the day I came out of my mother's womb.

Losing my grandmother this week, in conjunction with the extraordinary announcement by Attorney General Eric Holder, made for the kind of emotional cocktail that might possibly kill a man, like using uppers and downers while drinking a glass of Vodka. I don't drink or use drugs, but I think this might be how it feels.

In case you haven't noticed, Attorney General Eric Holder made one of the most impactful announcements in recent history on the effects of mass incarceration.

Holder expressed a commitment to making major adjustments in federal criminal policy, including getting rid of mandatory minimums for low-level, non-violent drug offenders. This will send fewer people to prison for long periods of time and also allow judges a greater degree of discretion to avoid the Draconian drug sentences that we've been seeing over the last 40 years.

> "Too many Americans go to too many prisons for far too long, and for no good law enforcement reason," Holder told the American Bar Association in San Francisco.

The United States incarcerates more citizens per capita than any country on earth. The federal prison population has grown by over 800 percent since 1980, with nearly half of those incarcerated being locked up for drug-related crimes. Prisons have become profitable, and corporations now earn billions of dollars each year by taking advantage of the loophole in the 13th Amendment which states that slavery is actually legal in the United States if you've been convicted of a crime.

As a professor of Finance, I must reiterate the dangers of building a capitalist model on the idea of incarceration. It leads us down a slippery slope where our society actually WANTS to put people in prison, since cheap labor allows the US to compete more effectively in the global economy. This is why it is no surprise that there are states across America that are taking money out of education and using those funds to build more prisons. A well-educated American doesn't make for a very good slave.

Making matters worse, a disproportionate number of these inmates are African American males. These men are the ones who were meant to be the husbands, fathers and leaders in our communities. Instead, these men were drafted away to modern day concentration camps for decades at a time for offenses that were no worse than what we see in Syracuse University frat houses every single weekend. If they were to apply stop-and-frisk to any college campus, thousands of white kids would be going to prison. These people aren't being put in prison camps in order to make our society safer.

Instead, our world is only made more dangerous after we take otherwise redeemable young people and turn them into killers, criminals, and in some cases, diseased men who become so marginalized that they live their lives with a death wish.

The HIV epidemic in the black community can be traced right back to the prisons, where men and women are raped on a regular basis. The mental illness crisis in our community is driven by mass amounts of incarceration, causing too many of our children to be forced to deal with that highly-disturbed uncle, brother or father who drowns out his problems with a liquor bottle or a crack pipe. The extreme growth in single parent homes is tied to mass incarceration, since it's difficult for women to find men to marry when so many of them are getting locked up. So, this isn't just a black male problem or an inmate problem: It's a problem for all of us.

I could go on and on, but the point is clear: The War on Drugs has destroyed our community in the same way that Hurricane Katrina took out the city of New Orleans. A generation later, an army of fatherless children roam the streets, some of whom become menaces to society before they leave the fifth grade. Even worse, the poison of prisons has marinated into our psyches, disguising itself as "black culture," showing up in our music, our dress code, and the way we speak to each other.

Letters like the one written by a young woman to the judge who gave her father 14 life sentences help us to see firsthand how mass incarceration has destroyed families and made our country worse off than before. Just last year, my heart bled as I watched my older brother figure (an uncle slightly older than me) die after decades of mental illness and substance abuse that I believe came from being sent to prison at an early age. Most of us have seen the impact of prisons in our own lives, and we know that not every person in prison is beyond redemption.

I must publicly express my most sincere appreciation to Attorney General Eric Holder for listening when Russell Simmons and I wrote our letter to President Barack Obama. The meetings weren't easy and I don't enjoy speaking to politicians, but Russell has taught me a lot about the power of diplomacy and effective expression. I'd also like to thank the celebrities, activists, scholars and public figures who signed the letter, along with the thousands of citizen soldiers who supported our petition.

It would be presumptuous of me to think that our letter was the sole reason that the attorney general made his announcement, but our coalition, consisting of supporters as diverse as Jamie Foxx, Brad Pitt, Michelle Alexander and Jesse Jackson, was strong enough to get us a meeting with the Attorney General's office. I was impressed, thrilled and inspired by the broad range of Americans who've come to understand the devastating impact of mass incarceration, and even people like Kim Kardashian, Justin Bieber, Lil Wayne and the presidents of Morehouse and

Spelman were willing to lend their names to the initiative. I didn't care if I agreed or disagreed with the people on the list: Our only objective was to accept the support of anyone willing to use their fan base to help with this important cause.

We couldn't have done this without you and I thank you from the bottom of my soul.

Eric Holder's words represent a huge victory for all of us. If followed by appropriate action, this decision will make our communities better, safer and more fulfilled in the long-run. Unborn children will enter a world that is a little less hurtful than the one we experienced during the dark era of mass incarceration. We may even one day be able to raise our children in a world that doesn't build a prison cell and casket for every black child on the day they are born. Our children deserve to live, prosper, succeed and be happy.

It's time to start the healing.

Black Buying Power Expected to Reach $1.1 Trillion Dollars

Black people have lots of money and we are determined to spend it. According to the State of the African-American Consumer Report, African American buying power is expected to rise to $1.1 trillion by 2015. This makes the black community a force to be reckoned with when it comes to the power of earning and consumption. The study was designed to analyze the buying and spending habits of the black community, likely so major corporations can figure out how we think and what we want to buy. The goal at the end of the day, is for corporations to find out how to get your money out of your pocket.

The results of the study were released at the 41st Annual Legislative Congressional Black Caucus Foundation Conference.

> "By sharing, for example, that African Americans over-index in several key areas, including television viewing and mobile phone usage," Susan Whiting, vice chair of information and analytics company Nielsen, told BlackVoices.com. "We've provided a better picture of where the African American

community can leverage that buying power to help their communities."

"Too often, companies don't realize the inherent differences of our community, are not aware of the market size impact and have not optimized efforts to develop messages beyond those that coincide with Black History Month," said NNPA chairman, Cloves Campbell. "It is our hope that by collaborating with Nielsen, we'll be able to tell the African American consumer story in a manner in which businesses will understand, and, that this understanding will propel those in the C-Suite to develop stronger, more inclusive strategies that optimize their market growth in Black communities, which would be a win-win for all of us."

The study concluded that if African-Americans were a country, we'd be 16th in the world in spending power. It also found that African Americans use our cell phones twice as much as whites. As a person who's taught Finance at the college level for nearly twenty years, here's what the study's results say to me:

1) **African Americans should be sure to harness our vast economic power by targeting our spending to**

black-owned businesses. This will help with the black unemployment problem by providing much-needed capital to black companies who can't get financing from traditional sources. White people have proven that they don't like to hire us. A recent experiment by a blogger (Yolanda Spivey) showed that when she changed her profile to appear to be a white woman, the number of job offers she received skyrocketed. This is the struggle we're dealing with, as Washington politicians love to assume that black people just don't want to work.

2) **We should all save and invest our money and not be duped into the "feel-good" domain of mass consumption.** Consumption is like alcohol or a drug: It intoxicates you into an addiction to short-term gratification that leads you to long-term economic slavery. We can't always focus on doing what feels good; we must instead focus on actions that provide a long-term benefit.

3) **We should remember that our financial independence is critical for our spiritual and social independence.** You can never demand your civil rights while simultaneously begging the descendants of your historical oppressors to help you feed your children. Malcolm X told us this long ago, and it's one of the reasons

that black America is so blatantly disrespected as a viable political constituency.

In a capitalist society, MONEY-IS-POWER. More importantly, it is the intelligent application of money that becomes critical to the survival and prosperity of our community. If you aren't smart enough to control the power of money, then the power of money will ultimately control you. Don't work hard to become a high-paid slave, for you deserve a better fate than that.

Jesse Jackson, Al Sharpton and the Black Agenda – It's Time for a Unified Front

Rev. Jesse Jackson pulled off something that the US State Department could not. The pastor and activist went across the world to Gambia and saved 38 lives in one meeting. Jackson met with Gambian President Yahya Jammeh, and was able to leave the country with Amadou Janneh and Tamsir Jasseh, two men who'd been incarcerated for treason after protesting against the government. The rest of the prisoners were also set to be executed, and Rev. Jackson got the president to reconsider his decision to move forward with the executions. His achievement was nothing short of phenomenal.

I spoke with Rev. Jackson this week while appearing on his radio show. We were all a bit surprised to see that none of the big three media outlets (ABC, NBC, CBS) covered his trip to Gambia. Surprisingly, only Fox News sent a correspondent to cover the negotiations. This surprised me, since Fox was the network that seemed determined to destroy Rev. Jackson back in 2008 when he was caught making problematic remarks about Barack Obama off the air. Maybe Rev. Jackson has forgiven Fox News for what they did, but I have not. At the same time, Rev. Jackson also takes responsibility for his mistake and has apologized multiple times.

I asked Rev. Jackson how he was able to go to Gambia and do something that the state department had been unable to do. Rev. Jackson mentioned that the civil rights movement had achieved a type of moral authority around the world that the US government does not possess. The model that African Americans used to obtain our rights within the United States has inspired the world, earning respect from leaders who appreciate what we've accomplished.

"I can have meetings with people who won't talk to anybody else," he said. "Our opinion matters in the world in a way that the government's opinion does not."

With regard to Rev. Jackson's achievement in Gambia, it is important that we support all black public figures who are seeking to make progress for people of color, even if they are not being invited to the White House. Part of the reason that such little progress has been made in the black community since the advent of the Obama presidency is that the powers that be have made people choose between those who are passively loyal to Obama and those who are loyal to black American issues. This should not be a decision that we are forced to make, for we are not betraying Barack Obama by asking him to address African American issues.

I've spent a great deal of time around both Rev. Jackson and Rev. Al Sharpton over the last four years, and both of them have been strong supporters and defenders of the president. The primary difference between the two is that Rev. Sharpton is taking Obama's agenda to black people and Rev. Jackson is taking the agenda of black people to the president. While some say that the black community has not been clear on what it would like President Obama to do, selective listening often leads to a set of conclusions that are patently false.

Rev. Jackson has been very consistent in asking the Obama Administration to address poverty, inequality and violence as part of the Democratic Party platform. Poverty is as bad as it's been since Dr. King was alive, economic and educational inequality still limit opportunities for our children and violence is killing our kids every day. I would personally add the mass incarceration epidemic to the mix, to argue that the black agenda has been presented loud and clear.

Given that a black agenda has been long presented to the White House, the primary question is "Which leadership is the Obama Administration listening to?"

Are they listening to black leaders who come to White House functions and fight for gay marriage, the Dream Act and other matters that have been handed down by the Obama Administration? Or are they listening to the leaders who have been consistently beating the drum on poverty, inequality, violence and mass incarceration? I argue that while the Obama Administration certainly has the right to have ideas of its own, we can no longer have black people wasting their votes by supporting an administration that uses this political capital to go fight for someone else. It is important to make it abundantly clear that there IS INDEED a black agenda, and that this agenda is just as important as anyone else's.

As we move forward to a second term for President Barack Obama, I remain hopeful that the president will understand the importance of sitting down with a multitude of African American leaders, and not just the ones with whom he feels most comfortable. Rev. Al Sharpton has been a great support mechanism for the administration, but meetings with Obama must also include Rev. Jesse Jackson, Dr. Julianne Malveaux, Dr. Wilmer Leon, Dr. Ron Daniels, Michelle Alexander, and perhaps even his old pastor, Jeremiah Wright. Meetings should include others who are in a position to intelligently discuss poverty, inequality, violence and mass incarceration in ways that are both understanding of presidential limitations, but substantive enough to encourage the White House to make these matters a priority.

We can't continue to allow ourselves to be bamboozled.

Father Michael Pfleger Says We Should Protect Black and Brown Kids From Guns Also

In this interview, Dr. Boyce Watkins speaks with Father Michael Pfleger of the St. Sabina Church on the Southside of Chicago. Father Pfleger has been a fierce advocate for equality and has long battled against discrimination. Father Pfleger says that the recent killings at Sandy Hook Elementary in Newtown, Connecticut should be a wake-up call about the dangers of making guns readily available to the public. He also notes the writing on the wall—that this violence meant very little to the nation when black children were being shot. A transcript of the interview is below:

Boyce: Hi, I'm Dr. Boyce Watkins from YourBlackWorld.com and anybody who follows anything that I do knows that there is one guy I respect probably as much as anybody on this planet and that is Father Michael Pfleger. He's the head of Saint Sabina in the south side of Chicago. He has been a relentless advocate for justice and equality throughout America not just for people of color, but for all people and he is a person who's willing to do what's necessary in order to do what's right. I've got father Pfleger on the line today and I want to ask father Pfleger, how are you doing today?

Pfleger: Great sir, and believe me the respect is mutual. I have tremendous respect for your voice and your courage and your willingness to continue to address issues and ask the hard questions. So I thank you for what you do.

Boyce: Thank you very much, thank you. Right now we're in the middle of a really interesting time in America. We just had a horrible tragedy take place in Connecticut. A lot of people are tentative about discussing one of the issues that you've been very consistent about which is dealing with gun violence and also gun control. Right after the incident took place, one of the things I really appreciated was on social media you immediately said something that I think a lot of people needed to hear in terms of what we need to do to deal with these kinds of situation and prevent them before they happen. Can you sir reiterate what your points were on that Facebook post?

Pfleger: Well, there are two things I think are absolutely important. First we have to address the culture of violence that has become a norm in this country that we are denying and that we are not facing head on. And that is we have a culture right now in America where the first line of violence. We've done this since 9/11, we've shown as a government that's what we do when we're mad at people we attack them. We send planes, we drop missiles, send bombs. I think we see it in the social media, we see it in TV shows, we see it in entertainment, we see it in video games, we see it in music and YouTube. So I see all this violence has become the culture of America. We saw it in the health care when 50 and 60 year old people were pushing each other in hearings and meetings. So that's one thing but the second thing is, this gun issue, this love affair of America with guns and this proliferation of guns, this easy access to guns. We are the most armed country in the world and we are seeing the effect of that. Until we deal head on with the gun issues and tell people all the time—I understand how the second amendment has been interpreted by the Supreme Court, fine. But we have to stop this easy access and this proliferation of guns, these loopholes, where nobody is held accountable with a gun. The fact is all these guns in Connecticut were bought legally.

So guns are being bought legally, sold on the streets, out of the trunks of cars. Given to anybody to use and there's no accountability. Assault weapons first of all and high magazines should be banned in this country. They are military weapons. How dare we ban them in Iraq but we won't ban them in our own country. These mass shootings are because we've allowed it in our country and that needs to be stopped immediately.

Secondly we need to deal with this love affair with guns. People cannot feel that anybody can get a gun whenever they want in this country and have no accountability. Somebody can go to a gun shop right now, buy 200 guns a week legally and sell them on the street and they're not held responsible. That's why we've been telling people to title a gun just like a car so there is a responsibility that comes with it just like a car. If you don't transfer a title then you're responsible for what happens to that gun. Close the loophole.

We have 120,000 people in Illinois named with mental illness, whose names are not even on the records. They can go buy a gun today and there's no accountability to them. You can sell it on the street or you can lose it and nobody holds you accountable to it. So until we deal with this gun issue—and they say "it's not the gun it's the person with the gun." So here's just an example. If we have a staircase, on top of the staircase is a skateboard and you have to teach your child to stay away from the skateboard by the staircase you could end up killing yourself or hurting yourself badly. I have to teach my child that. But as adults we also have responsibility to remove the skateboard from the staircase. And that's what we have to do now. We move the guns from this easy access in America. Where anybody can get it, anybody can use it and they're not held accountable.

So until we deal with the gun issue I think personally that a big part of the problem is that all our public leaders around this country getting out and talking about their sympathy and what happened in Connecticut. My response is that if you do not do something to prevent the next Connecticut or the next Virginia, the next mall shooting or Aurora Theater shooting or the Gabby Gifford or the streets of Chicago. If you don't have the courage to do something to prevent it, then I'm just saying that your sympathy is shallow, it's phony and it's cheap. It's easy to be sorry, it's courage to say "we are going to in the name of these children stop this and contain what happens in this country."

Boyce: Alright I know that you're about to head off to go and actually give out some meals to some families today, which is a typical day for you because you're usually doing something for the community every day. One of the things I think people should know is that in the community that you serve, you've seen this kind of violence on a regular basis for a very long time. And the country hasn't necessarily responded in a way that they should. What do you think it is that exists in our nation that allows us to ignore so much of the violence that might take place in urban communities and then suddenly become aware when it happens to someone else. It's almost as if when this happened in Connecticut—it's as if it's the first time a child had ever been shot before. We know that there are babies dying all over the neighborhoods across America. We know that babies are dying in Iraq and Palestine and other places. Where do you think that gap in the sensitivity comes from?

Pfleger: Well I think the other issue that we continue to avoid in America is we are afraid to have an honest conversation about race. We have nearly 500 people murdered in Chicago this year and hundreds of them children and teenagers and it has been basically dismissed across America. The number one issue of violence and the victims of violence in this country have been black or brown. And so America says "well it's those communities, it's those people of this, that's how it is in those neighborhoods." And they have dismissed it and they have turned their heads and walked away from it.

Twenty innocent children in Connecticut get killed and all of a sudden it's an American focus and it should be. All I say is that it also should be when it's in Chicago or Oakland or Newark or Philly or anyplace else in this country. Violence is the undeclared war, it's an epidemic in America and because the victims are primarily black and brown we've ignored it. I've said this for years and will continue to say it. It's going to happen just like it did with drugs when it was only in the black community nobody cared. When it grew into the homes and backyard of the children of Senators and Congressmen and Elected Officials, we had a war on drugs. Understand until we see this as a human problem, not a black or brown problem, and right now we've seen it's a human problem. I'm not quite sure and I say this with great hurt and pain but I'm not sure that if 20 children were murdered in the South side of Chicago or South Philly or South Central we would have the same national response. That's something that we have to deal with in this country.

But the reality is, this tragedy has happened. Let's use this moment to say you care about those children. Then let's care about children everywhere. Let's care about violence everywhere and let's decide that this human family has a sickness, a cancer that's destroying it across this country.

We cannot just deal with the symptom. Connecticut is a symptom, Arizona is a symptom and Chicago is a symptom. Let's deal with the root causes of guns and violence and a culture that we've developed in America and race that sits in the middle of it. Let's deal with it and let's say not just the next child in Connecticut but say the next child in America.

Boyce: Alright, well said. I want to say thank you very much for your time Father Pfleger. I really appreciate it.

Pfleger: Thank you doctor. I appreciate all you're doing and thanks for your great work and always thanks for your support.

Boyce: Well, thank you, thank you. It means a lot brother. You know when you and I had a chance to talk a few weeks ago, I told my friend it's sort of like talking to an older brother. You know an older brother who says "Look this is what I've done over the last 30 years...[Laughter] I need you to take this baton and keep running alongside me." So your example is one that inspires a lot of us and that spirit is something that I believe will live forever. So God bless you.

Pfleger: Well thank you sir and bless you man. Appreciate it and have a blessed Christmas.

Boyce: Thank you, thank you. Thank you all for checking us out at YourBlackWorld.com and remember that caring about the children in Connecticut also means that we need to care about the children everywhere. So let's use this situation to make sure that those babies didn't die in vain. We can save those other children out there who are going to meet an unfortunate fate if we fail to act today. There's a child out there somewhere now whose life is in jeopardy because something is going to happen to that child if we don't stop the forces of evil in our world that are designed to take a child's future away from him or her. So we've got to act and we can't just sit back and be polite about it. We've got to go out and do what needs to be done. Till we meet again. Please stay strong, be blessed and be educated. We are gone.....Peace.

Michelle Alexander Agrees: Reparations Should Be Paid for the Failed War on Drugs

The other day, I mentioned that it makes sense for black America to call for reparations for the War on Drugs. This misleading assault on the economic and social stability of black America has led to untold devastation in our communities, as drugs and guns were allowed to flood urban areas. This was not by accident, as the CIA looked the other way and allowed the drugs to come into our neighborhoods to fund covert and illegal wars overseas.

As a result, families were torn apart by addiction, homicide rates flew through the roof, and black America has been at the receiving end of a mass incarceration epidemic of holocaust proportions. Given that it has been proven that government officials played a direct role in the creation of this madness, I say that there is a logical argument for reparations.

I spoke with Ohio State University Law Professor Michelle Alexander, author of the book, *The New Jim Crow*, and she agrees with this assessment. Alexander's book is a telling and riveting reminder of the horrific impact that mass incarceration has had on black America. "I think it's a powerful point you're making," she said. Adding:

> "Also, I think it's worth noting that the US has spent more than one trillion dollars waging the drug war since it began-funds that could have been used for education, job creation, etc. It is reasonable that at least a trillion dollars be paid to repair the damage that has been done, reparations that could take the form of massive investments in the schools and community hardest hit by the drug war, as well as payments to individuals and families that have been destroyed."

Are reparations practical? I am not sure, given that we live in a nation that has refused to even apologize for slavery. But the fact that an entity refuses to take responsibility for its actions does not mean that you should not accurately highlight such accountability. Those who expect America to calm itself into a sweet, kind "post-racial society" must be made aware that unforgiveable amounts of damage has been done as a result of the war on drugs, and any post-racial society must be built on accepting responsibility for wrongs that have been committed in the past.

The War on Drugs is not like slavery, which affected our great, great, great grandparents. Many children today have parents who've received 60-year prison sentences for drug possession. Families are mourning the loss of loved ones who've been murdered by weapons allowed to enter black communities as a result of the drug trade. I run into countless young people who are traumatized after growing up with parents who were addicted to drugs. The pain and misery is all around us, so it's very simple to prove that the damage has been nothing short of crippling.

It's time to address this matter in a series of public forums, legislation, petitions and even protests. It's also time for all of us to promote awareness in our own communities about the dangers of drugs and mentor our young people to create better lives for themselves. Like a town that's been ravaged by a violent tornado, it's going to take a consistent effort by all of us to clean up the mess in our community. It's time to start making things right.

5 Things I Learned from the Great Malcolm X

Happy birthday Malcolm. Malcolm X, arguably the greatest black man who ever lived (even without being elected to public office), has become a mere afterthought in mainstream American history. His grave site is shameful, and almost none of us know the day he was born. The neglect of Malcolm's legacy makes it clear that America doesn't love him as much as the more digestible Martin Luther King Jr.

Being unloved can actually be a good thing. Malcolm was feared by the establishment, and fear can be more powerful than love because sometimes your enemies can respect you more than your friends. The so-called "love" we received via friendly, polite integration has left us consistently disrespected by even our own black politicians. Malcolm taught us how be truly powerful, which is why White America never programmed you to accept him.

To celebrate what Malcolm left us with (much of which has been forgotten), I thought I'd lay out five things I learned from the life of Malcolm X:

1) **The Value of True Independence:** In our quest for integration, we quickly learned that it's hard to earn respect in a capitalist society when you aren't prepared to be self-sufficient. Freedom is not the same as independence: A man can be free to do whatever he wants, but if he's not independent, he'll end up going right back to his oppressor to get the things he needs in order to survive. That is what millions of black people are doing to this very day – we line up for jobs with companies not owned by us, and wonder why our unemployment rate is double that of White America. Malcolm warned us that this was going to happen, but many of us failed to listen.

2) **Self-respect:** You don't need anyone to validate you with a fancy job title, a high income or a big house, especially if you must sacrifice your integrity in order to get them. You were already a valuable person on the day you were born. This is an important lesson to remember in a world where even our most powerful black public figures continue to seek mainstream validation in order to feel significant. When your adversary knows that you need him to pat you on the head in order for you to feel good about yourself, then he will always control the limitations of your possibilities.

3) **The Necessity for Intelligence and Education:** Intelligence and education are not one in the same, but both serve as armor for people of color in a world that is designed to destroy them. The worst thing that any man or woman can do is walk away from education, because when you do that, you are walking right into the grasp of slavery. Not only do black people need to embrace education, we must demand educational excellence from our children, where they pursue academic achievement with as much passion as they have when chasing after tickets to the next Lil Wayne concert. In addition to being formally educated, young people should be taught to seek knowledge from independent sources and to engage in critical thinking. If you can't formulate your own opinion about the world, someone is always happy to give your opinion to you.

4) **The Importance of Spiritual and Physical Health:** This isn't something you get from eating and consuming the food and ideas being fed to you by the descendants of your historical oppressors. Every day, your mind and body are being polluted by music teaching black men to murder one another, food that makes you obese, and media images designed to turn you into a greedy, selfish, capitalistic c**n (see "n****z in Paris" as a case-in-point).

It is critical to rise above this psychological poison, for it is essential for our very survival.

5) **The Value of True Courage:** Capacity, success, wealth, education and power mean almost nothing without the desire to commit to a cause greater than yourself. Part of what made Malcolm every bit as great as Martin Luther King (without all the white American fanfare) is that he figured out that, even in death, he could live forever by injecting the next generation with a spiritual energy that will exist for thousands of years. We are all his children, and he lives through us. His power and vision will live far longer than his physical body ever could.

In fact, Malcolm X will never die.

About The Author

Dr. Boyce D. Watkins is one of the leading financial scholars and social commentators in America. He advocates for education, economic empowerment and social justice and has changed the definition of what it means to be a Black scholar and leader in America.

He is one of the founding fathers of the field of Financial Activism – The objective of creating social change through the use of conscientious capitalism. He is a Blue Ribbon Speaker with Great Black Speakers, Inc. and one of the most highly sought after public figures in the country.

In addition to publishing a multitude of scholarly articles on finance, education and black social commentary, Dr. Watkins has presented his message to millions, making regular appearances in various national media outlets, including CNN, Good Morning America, MSNBC, FOX News, BET, NPR, Essence Magazine, USA Today, The Today Show, ESPN, The Tom Joyner Morning Show and CBS Sports.

Educationally, Dr. Watkins earned BA and BS degrees with a triple major in Finance, Economics and Business Management. In college, he was selected by the Wall Street Journal as the Outstanding Graduating Senior in Finance. He then earned a Masters Degree in Mathematical Statistics from University of Kentucky and a PhD in Finance from Ohio State University and was the only African-American in the world to earn a PHD in Finance during the year 2002. He is the founder of The Black Wealth Bootcamp, The Black Business School and The Your Black World coalition, which have a collective total of 300,000 subscribers and 1.4 million social media followers world-wide.

Made in the USA
Middletown, DE
24 November 2022

15878508R00208